AVISSON YOUNG ADULT SERIES

Here Comes Eleanor

A NEW BIOGRAPHY OF ELEANOR ROOSEVELT
for young people

Virginia Veeder Westervelt

D0916130

Avisson Press Inc.
Greensboro

First edition
Printed in the United States of America
ISBN 1-888105-33-X

Library of Congress Cataloging-in-Publication Data

Westervelt, Virginia Veder,
    Here comes Eleanor ; a new biography of Eleanor Roosevelt for young people / Virginia Veder Westervelt -- 1st ed.
    p.   cm. -- (Avisson young adult series)
    Includes bibliographical references and index.
    Summary: A biography of the first wife of a president to have a public life and career of her own, devoted to helping others and working for peace.
    ISBN 1-888105-33-X (pbk.)
    1. Roosevelt, Eleanor, 1884-1962 --Juvenile literature.
2. Presidents' spouses--United States--Biography--Juvenile literature. [1. Roosevelt, Eleanor, 1884-1962. 2. Fi
3. Women--Biography.] I. Title. II. Series.
E807. 1.R48W44 1998
973.917 ' 092--dc21
[b]

Photo credits: All photos are courtesy of the Franklin D. Roosevelt Library.

Material from *Eleanor and Franklin,* © 1971 and *Eleanor, The Years Alone,* © 1972 by Joseph P. Lash is reprinted by permission of W.W. Norton Co., Publishers. Material from *This Is My Story* © 1939 and *This I Remember* © 1949, by Eleanor Roosevelt is reprinted by permission of Harper Collins, Publishers.

TO MY DAUGHTER
DEIDRE WESTERVELT MEEHAN
For her lively interest
And sustaining love

This I believe with all my heart:
If we want a free and peaceful world,
if we want to make the deserts bloom
and man to grow in greater dignity
as a human being,
we can do it.

—Eleanor Roosevelt

Acknowledgments

In trying to present an accurate picture of Eleanor Roosevelt's life, I am grateful to many authors for their insights into the personality and accomplishments of this remarkable woman, especially Joseph Lash's biographies and his editing of her letters, Elliott and James Roosevelt's interpretation of their family life, and Eleanor Roosevelt's autobiographies, other books and articles she wrote, and countless columns of "My Day."

The archivists of the Franklin D. Roosevelt Museum and Library have been generous in opening their files of Roosevelt letters and other material, and I thank them for invaluable help in allowing me to quote from letters and diary entries.

Several friends were happy to tell me of meetings with her.

I want especially to thank my friend, Mary Lou Colbert Neale, for sharing a letter she received from Eleanor about becoming a writer. Despite her busy schedule in her first year at the White House, she took the time to answer the query from an unknown young woman, "A writer must not only learn the technique of writing, but also learn something about life so that she may have something to say." And she added a postscript in her own writing, inviting the talented student, then a sophomore majoring in English Composition, to come to tea and bring some of her work for an honest appraisal.

Eleanor Roosevelt's friends wrote about her, giving me additional facets of her personality as they experienced it.

I have not wanted to clutter the story with footnotes, but each quotation is used with reference to its source, (e.g., "In her column for that day, Eleanor wrote . . .")

Since I grew up near Albany, New York, and have visited many countries that welcomed Eleanor on her travels, I could visualize her in Washington Park, Japan, Istanbul, etc.)

With anyone as prominent as the Roosevelts, there is so much material one is forced to choose certain incidents and to leave out others of perhaps equal importance. The choice has been mine and the interpretation, mine. I can only hope Eleanor would have approved.

Contents

Introduction

Rarely does a life, particularly that of a woman, affect the future of the world as did Eleanor Roosevelt's.

What was she really like and how did she get to be that way?

How did a shy, awkward, unhappy, self-conscious girl who felt incapable of doing anything, emerge from that stifling cocoon?

What gave someone who felt unloved and unlovable the confidence to become beloved?

How did she cope with disillusionment, disappointment, frustrations? What were her strengths and weaknesses? Her life had as many facets as an exquisitely cut diamond.

It was a long journey to her position as First Lady of the Land and later to the United Nations and the struggle for a workable Human Rights Declaration. The way Eleanor learned to meet her problems serves as an inspiration to many.

Through it all was her basic need to love and be loved, to feel that she was being useful, to find a way to put her ideals into action, her ideals for justice, decency, equality of women, civil rights, human rights, education, politics, freedom.

She found that way, for she believed in the power of individuals, working together, to right the wrongs and to transform society.

When polls were taken of the most admired women in the world, Eleanor Roosevelt consistently led the list. In one group of names of those having the most influence worldwide, no American Presidents were listed, but the name of Eleanor Roosevelt was there.

She was a feminist in the best sense of the word, urging women to have lives, interests, and personalities of their own apart from their traditional roles as wife, mother, and housekeeper.

She urged young people to believe in themselves, to be persistent in pursuing a dream, to have compassion for those in need and, perhaps more important, to take some action to help.

She expressed her philosophy in her life, and that life can bring encouragement to anyone who shares her feeling that "in spite of timidity and fear, in spite of a lack of special talents, one can find a way to live widely and fully. You have to accept whatever comes, and the only important thing is that you meet it with courage and with the best that you have to give."

Virginia Veeder Westervelt
Redlands, California

Chapter 1
The World of the Roosevelts

"I was more afraid of not being loved than of anything else," Eleanor Roosevelt wrote about her childhood. Her parents, Elliott and Anna Roosevelt, had wanted a boy, but on October 11, 1884, they produced a girl, and a scrawny one at that. Her father wrote to a friend that their first child, whom they named Anna Eleanor, was "a more wrinkled and less attractive baby than the average."

Her mother, Anna Hall Roosevelt, was still beautiful and had been what her social group called "a belle of society." The Halls came from a distinguished Hudson Valley family. (One of her ancestors, Robert R. Livingston, had helped draft the Declaration of Independence and had administered the oath of office to President George Washington.)

But no one said little Eleanor looked like her mother. When she was two, she had to wear a steel brace to straighten her spine, and her teeth stuck out like a beaver's. She overheard someone say she was "the Ugly Duckling." Not having read Hans Christian Anderson's story, she did not know that the duckling became a swan.

All Eleanor knew was that her mother laughed at her and called her "Granny," because "she is so funny and old fashioned." Eleanor remembered later that "my mother was troubled by my lack of beauty. I knew it as a child senses such things. She tried hard to bring me up so that my manners would compensate for my looks, but her efforts only made me more keenly conscious of my shortcomings."

Eleanor tried to make up for her plainness by being an obedient child, running errands and helping others in order to win a word of praise. Throughout her life, she never lost that urge for service. Her earliest ambition was to become a nurse.

Only her father never criticized her for being awkward, shy, or too solemn. And she adored him. To her, he was always the romantic adventurer just returned from Big Game hunting with his brother Theodore. He called Eleanor "Little Nell," after Dickens' character in "The Old Curiosity Shop," or sometimes "Father's Little Golden Hair."

Elliott Roosevelt, like his wife Anna Hall, also bore a name that had earned respect. The first Roosevelt in the New World, Claes Martenszen van Rosenvelt (Nicholas, son of Martin of the Rose Field) settled in New Amsterdam, later New York City, in the 1640s. His son Nicholas had two sons, James and John. John's branch became known as the Oyster Bay Roosevelts because they settled in Oyster Bay, Long Island.

Elliott's father, Theodore, Sr., was one of the founders of the Metropolitan Museum of Art and the Museum of Natural History. Elliott's brother, Theodore Roosevelt, Jr., became the "Rough Rider" of the Spanish-American War and later President of the United States.

James' descendants became wealthy landowners with estates high above the Hudson River. Among them, six generations later, was Franklin Delano Roosevelt, who became Eleanor's husband (and also President of the United States)!

The Oyster Bay and the Hyde Park Roosevelts traveled in the same social circles, both members of the "400," prominent families in New York who controlled social customs. Eleanor grew up used to servants, to trips to Europe, to tutors and governesses, to a house in town and one outside of the city for vacations.

Eleanor's mother's mother, Grandma Hall, had a summer

place called Tivoli, where Eleanor liked to ride the pony her father had given her. But she was so unsure of herself she never tried to make the pony go where she wanted, but let him choose his own path.

Yet Eleanor had a mind of her own if she felt strongly about something. Once in Italy she came back walking from a donkey ride, with the bare-footed donkey boy riding. She explained she couldn't stand it to see the boy's cut and bleeding feet grow more painful while she rode. And although the boy protested, she insisted he ride because her sturdy shoes would protect her. Her sympathy for others would always result in some action to relieve their problems.

But Eleanor could do little to help the situation at home. Her father often suffered from severe headaches, and to dull the pain he turned to alcohol. He tried several hospitals for "cures," but any benefit was short lived. (Many years later Eleanor's son Elliott would advance the theory, never satisfactorily proved, that his grandfather had had a brain tumor, "suffering constantly increasing agony . . . and turned to alcohol . . . to alleviate the pain."

Eleanor had no idea why he was away from home so much. Her mother told her only that he was sick and had gone South to try to get better. She missed his warmth and love. There were two brothers now, little Elliott and baby Hall. It was easy to see that her mother loved the boys, for she held them on her lap and hugged them as she had never done for Eleanor.

But one day Anna became ill. It was typhoid, they said, and in those days there wasn't much a doctor could do. Some people got well and some didn't. Anna Roosevelt died on December 7, 1892. Eleanor was eight years old. She knew she should feel sad, but her mother had always been cold and distant, so her death only meant that now her father would come home.

An early picture of Eleanor at age four, taken in New York City in April 1889.

He was dressed all in black when he came, told her soberly how much he had loved her mother, how he wished he could make up to her any sorrows he had caused. Then he took Eleanor for a drive, promising that someday she "would make a home for him again. We'll travel together and have a life of our own."

He did not stay long, however, for Anna had made her mother the children's guardian, and they were to live with her and her grown children still at home most of the time: Aunt Edith, Elizabeth (Aunt Tissie), Aunt Maude, Uncle Valentine (Vallie), and Uncle Edward, her mother's brothers and sisters.

The New York townhouse was a dreary place, filled with heavy furniture and dark draperies. The aunts and uncles were absorbed with their own affairs and had little time for the children. Yet Eleanor wrote years later, "I marvel at their sweetness, for never by word or deed did any of them make us feel that we were not in our own home."

Eleanor's father's letters filled her life. He told her how much he loved his "sweet daughter," urging her to write to him often, to be a good girl, not to give any trouble, to study hard, and to grow up into a woman he could be proud of.

From that time on, Eleanor lived in a dream world where her father was the gallant hero and she the heroine. When she walked with her French governess to classes in a friend's home, she pretended her father was beside her. When she wanted something and her grandmother said "No," she was sure her father would have said "Yes." She learned not to ask for anything so she would not be disappointed.

But Eleanor did not outwardly rebel. She wore without complaint the long black stockings, high buttoned shoes, and flannel underwear Grandma Hall thought necessary. She was supposed to take a cold sponge bath every morning, but she often cheated by getting the maid to pour in some hot water.

The next winter both little Elliott and Hall were ill with scarlet fever. Hall got well, but Ellie did not. Eleanor was sent to a cousin's and later wrote her father as she had been taught, "Our Lord wants Ellie boy with him now. We must

Eleanor (right) in an 1892 photograph with her father and brothers, Elliott (left) and G. Hall.

be happy and do God's will and we must cheer others."

Eleanor longed for her father, and he would have come oftener if Mrs. Hall had allowed him to. But when he did come there were frightening times. He took Eleanor to his club one day and left her in the coat room for six hours. She was afraid he had abandoned her, but finally she saw him being carried out, and the doorman took her home.

Then would come his letters full of excuses and promises, saying, "No other little girl will ever take your place in my heart. Maybe soon I'll come back well and strong and we will have such good times together like we used to have. . . . Try to be fair, honest, interesting, the kind of person you want to be; what other people say about you won't matter."

Eleanor remembered his advice all her life, particularly when she became a public figure and some people criticized everything she did.

His last letter told her he had been ill and not able to move from his bed for days. But he asked her about her pony and sent his affection. Three days later Mrs. Hall had to tell Eleanor that her father had died. And afterwards she wrote to Elliott's sister Corinne, "Poor child, she has had so much sorrow crowded into her short life, she now takes everything very quietly. The only remark she made was I did want to see Father once more.'"

Mrs. Hall felt that Eleanor, at ten, was too young to attend the funeral, so it was hard for her to believe her father was really dead. She went back into that dream world where her father was with her and just the two of them would have a wonderful life together.

On the surface Eleanor went to French classes, music classes, and a dancing class, enduring braces on her prominent teeth and feeling lonely, awkward and conscious of not being like other more attractive girls. Her grandmother dressed her like a child even when she became a teenager. Her dresses hung straight from her tall shoulders and were always too short.

But Eleanor tried to follow her father's advice. She wrote in her journal, "I try to be good and sweet and quiet, but I have not succeeded. . . . I never succeed in doing what I mean to do. I can feel in me sometimes that I can do much more than I am doing, and I mean to try until I do succeed."

Eleanor was allowed to go only to family parties, and she looked forward to visiting Uncle Theodore and his family at

14

Oyster Bay, for here everything was fun and exciting. Teddy Roosevelt reminded Eleanor of her father as he had been when he was younger. Later she wrote, "I loved chasing through the hay stacks in the barn with Uncle Ted after us, and going up to the gun room on the top floor of the house where Uncle Ted would read aloud, chiefly poetry."

Or they would run down a steep hill into the sea, playing follow the leader with Uncle Ted. Eleanor was terrified, but she plunged down the cliff with the others. She had been afraid of the sea ever since the ship her family took to Europe had been rammed by another ship in the fog. In the excitement Eleanor became separated from her parents who had been lowered over the side in a lifeboat. Someone dropped the frightened child into her father's arms and she was safe, but she never forgot the terror of that experience. Writing about it later, she also remembered being afraid of many other things, "of the dark, of displeasing people, of failure."

Eleanor was even a little afraid of her strong-willed cousin Alice, though she admired her. Alice never seemed as fond of Eleanor and made fun of her solemn, goody-goody attitude. "I was made to feel," Eleanor wrote years later, "that nothing about me would attract attention or would bring me admiration." And this, of course, she longed for.

At one family dance party, however, as Eleanor sat on the sidelines, she caught the eye of her distant cousin Franklin just finishing a dance with vivacious cousin Alice. Eleanor looked away, but Franklin strode across the room and stopped, smiling, in front of her and asked her to dance.

Eleanor got up quickly, though sure that this tall, poised young man had only asked her out of pity. But she loved to dance and "was grateful to be rescued from the sidelines." Franklin was full of chatter about Groton School and his plans for Harvard. Eleanor was a good listener but felt she never knew what to say to boys. But Franklin, after all, was family, however distant, and she discovered she could talk easily enough to him.

He reminded Eleanor of the time when she was two and he was four years old. He had crawled around the nursery with Eleanor on his back one day when Eleanor and her mother had visited at Hyde Park. When the music stopped, he told Eleanor how much he had enjoyed the dance and hoped he'd see her at another party soon. He told his mother the next day, "Cousin Eleanor has a good mind."

But it was to be four years before they met again. Eleanor's life was due for a drastic change. Her Auntie Bye, her father's sister, whom Eleanor considered "one of the most interesting women I have ever known," had attended a school in Paris run by Mademoiselle Marie Souvestre. The boarding school for girls had now been moved to the outskirts of London. Auntie Bye suggested to Mrs. Hall that it was time Eleanor had some formal schooling. Although she spoke French with the perfect accent of her French governess and she loved to read, her knowledge of academic subjects was slight.

In the society in which she grew up, Eleanor was taught that all a girl needed was good manners, definite ideas of right and wrong, and the obligation to be of good Christian service to others. Women had no rights of their own apart from their roles as wife, mother, or daughter. They couldn't vote, own property, or handle their own money. Eleanor was destined to play an important part in changing these limitations, though she could scarcely have imagined how this was to come about.

Allenswood, Mlle. Souvestre's school, opened a new life for Eleanor. Though she carried a packet of her father's letters with her and read them over and over to keep him close, she soon became involved in school activities. Lonely and shy, without a close family of her own, she felt the school became that family and Mlle. Souvestre the loving, wise parent she needed.

A vigorous women in her seventies with ideas ahead of her time, Mlle. "Sou," as the girls called her, was responsible for giving Eleanor a sense of her own worth. She recognized depths in Eleanor that had long been imprisoned and wanted to set free her mind and personality.

"Think for yourself," she taught the girls. She did not want her students to give back what the textbooks said. "Make up your own mind," she would say, "and use your knowledge to help others who are too poor or too ignorant to help themselves. Make your life count for something."

She grew fond of Eleanor, and took her on a vacation trip to the Continent. Pretending she didn't want to be bothered, she asked Eleanor to make all the arrangements, look up time tables, hotels, and sightseeing trips.

At the turn of the century when young ladies required chaperones for every occasion, Mlle. Souvestre encouraged Eleanor to poke around European cities by herself, seeing whatever interested her. Eleanor gained in self-assurance every day. Thinking about the experience later she wrote, "I was sixteen years old, keener than I have probably ever been since, and more alive to beauty. I sallied forth to see Florence (Italy) alone."

Eleanor was popular with the other girls at school, "beloved by everybody," her cousin Corinne reported, always ready to listen to someone else's problems but seldom talking about her own. For the first time she heard the girls compliment her on her shining hair, her expressive grey-blue eyes, her graceful hands. She could hardly believe they were talking about her.

Eleanor spent three years there and wanted to return for a fourth and then go on to college. Mlle. Sou encouraged her

A school photo of Eleanor, taken circa 1898 in New York City.

and wrote to Mrs. Hall that Eleanor "showed a rare purity of spirit," that she was straightforward and honest and had "a sympathy for all those who live with her."

But Grandmother Hall had decided since Eleanor was eighteen she must bow to social custom and "come out" in society. Eleanor had no interest in the round of social teas, dances, and parties that were required of New York debutantes in their social circle, but it never occurred to her to disobey her grandmother's decision.

Eleanor came home, was "introduced to society," and dutifully made the rounds, but she felt some of the parties were "utter agony. I knew I was the first girl in my mother's family who was not a 'belle,' and though I never acknowledged it to any of them at the time, I was deeply ashamed." She was invited to parties because her name was on the favored list, but in spite of the fact that she had gained in self-confidence, she never really enjoyed the social life, feeling she was wasting time when Mlle. Souvestre had said she should make something of her life.

Home had become increasingly difficult as Uncle Vallie became drunk and obnoxious, sometimes even dangerous as he would take pot shots at guests when they approached the house. Eleanor, naturally enough, was afraid of him when he had been drinking. While her grandmother stayed with him at Tivoli, Eleanor went to the New York house to live with her Aunt Edith, who was always just starting or getting over a new love affair. She was moody and self-absorbed. Hall had been sent off to school at Groton.

Eleanor visited him when she could. But as a member of the Junior League she was supposed to become interested in some charitable cause. She worked at the Rivington Settlement House teaching dancing and gymnastics and taking the girls on excursions to museums or the beach.

The Junior Leaguers also invited the girls' parents to the settlement house to urge them to demand more rights for women, shorter hours, better pay, and to get into politics to work for better schools and safer streets. Eleanor also joined the Consumers' League, looking into working conditions in garment factories and stores.

Eleanor's work became more important to her than the butterfly social life she was supposed to lead. It was the kind of work Mlle. Sou had considered vital, fighting for the rights of those who could not fight their own battles. Eleanor remembered Mlle. Sou's belief that each individual had a responsibility to leave the world better than she found it, to use her education and knowledge to help others. She had always enjoyed being useful, and helping those less fortunate became one of the guiding principles of her life.

At this time Franklin appeared again. He traveled in the same orbit, they saw each other at parties, and Franklin made no secret of the fact that he thought Eleanor attractive with her red-gold hair, keen mind, and sympathetic personality. He asked her to house parties at his Hyde Park home and was soon coming down frequently from Harvard to take her to parties, picnics, boating expeditions, and long walks. Franklin's diary reported that he saw Eleanor at the House Show, and two weeks later he "lunched with Eleanor," or shopped with his mother but escaped "for tea with Eleanor."

He went to the White House for afternoon tea with Alice Roosevelt, whose father was now President, and discovered that Eleanor was also a guest. They all "dined with Uncle Ted," and then "went to the theater and sat near Eleanor." He got his mother to invite her to his twenty-first birthday party, and at the end of June, a house party at Hyde Park.

But for so long Eleanor had thought herself unattractive, uninteresting, and unloved, she couldn't believe Franklin was serious. In fact, one day when he picked her up at the Settlement House, the girls giggled and asked her if handsome Franklin was "her feller." She had never thought of him as a "boyfriend," but only as a distant cousin who was being nice to her. "The idea that you would permit any man to kiss you before you were engaged to him never crossed my mind," she confessed later.

"I had painfully high ideals and a tremendous sense of duty, entirely unrelieved by any sense of humor or any appreciation of the weaknesses of human nature. Things were either right or wrong to me," she said about herself when she became more mature.

Franklin was equally conventional. His father was many

Eleanor in fashionable turn-of-the-century attire, Summer 1900.

years older than Franklin's mother, Sara. He was president of a small railroad, bred trotting horses, managed a large farm, and was active in local affairs of Dutchess County. His fortune was large enough to let him live the comfortable life of a country squire.

Franklin's mother was a Delano, wealthy in her own right and with very definite ideas of what was "proper and fitting." She liked to tell the story of an ocean voyage they had taken when Franklin was just a baby. A storm came up, water seeped into the cabin, and when it reached the edge of a fur coat hanging by her berth, she took the coat, wrapped it around the baby, and said to Franklin's father, "Poor little boy; if we must go down, he is going down warm." She never lost that urge to protect "her boy."

So Franklin was brought up in a loving but strict environment where he could have anything he wanted as long as his parents approved. He was in love and he wanted to marry Eleanor. By the time he proposed, he had convinced her he loved her very much. She accepted, as she said later, "because it seemed an entirely natural thing to do." And she added unromantically, "I had a great curiosity about life and a desire to participate in every experience that might be the lot of women . . . I felt the urge to be a part of the stream of life."

In other words, Eleanor was young, she wanted marriage and children, Franklin was handsome and attentive, and she felt at ease with him. When her grandmother asked her if she was really in love, she said in her autobiography, "I solemnly answered 'yes,' and yet I know that it was years later before I understood what being in love was or what loving really meant."

In fact, when someone asked Eleanor, years later, what was the best age to marry, she answered, "I should feel that it was a mistake to marry too early before one's character has had an opportunity to develop, but between the ages of twenty and twenty-five seems to me good."

Chapter 2
Marriage, Children, and Complications

Franklin did not tell his mother until Thanksgiving, knowing instinctively that she would disapprove. Since his elderly father's death, Franklin's mother had seen to it that she and her son were closer than ever. Sara had great plans for her only son which did not include marriage for many years. When he was in Harvard, she had taken an apartment in Cambridge to be near him. She planned that he would go to Columbia Law School, and after they had traveled the globe together, Franklin would return to Hyde Park to be the country squire his father had been.

"Franklin gave me quite a startling announcement," she wrote in her journal when he told her he wanted to marry Eleanor. Since they were so young (Eleanor was nineteen and he was twenty-one), she persuaded them to keep their engagement secret for a year. Following his graduation, she took Franklin and his roommate on a Caribbean cruise.

Eleanor did not record her reaction to Franklin's obvious pleasure at the idea of the voyage, but she did note that when he returned he told her about dancing with "lots of pretty girls. But not one of them could hold a candle to you."

During the year of waiting, Eleanor had other suitors, which she dutifully and somewhat teasingly reported to Franklin. "Never have I known anyone able to talk the steady stream that Nick Biddle does." And when a cousin thought Eleanor was too indifferent to Franklin, she wrote him, "they thought I did not realize how serious you might be, and I led them on very wickedly and made believe I was much worried at the thought that you might really care for me in more than a friendly way! May I be forgiven for all my white lies, but it seems like I can't help doing it."

The year of waiting did nothing to discourage the young couple, and they announced their engagement in the autumn of 1904. Eleanor, anxious to please Franklin's mother, wrote her, "I know just how you feel and how hard it must be, but I do so want you to learn to love me a little. You must know that I will always try to do what you wish, for I have grown to love you very much." Since her own mother had never shown her much affection, Eleanor hungered for a mother's love.

By this time Eleanor had convinced herself that she loved Franklin with utter devotion. She wrote him, "I love you, dearest, and I hope that I shall always prove worthy of the love which you have given me. I have never known before what it was to be absolutely happy." And in another letter she confessed, "I am so happy, oh, so happy, and I love you so much."

Franklin wrote to all of his friends and received letters of congratulation, all of which he kept. Cousin Lyman Delano wrote, "I have more respect and admiration for Eleanor than any girl I have ever met and have always thought that the man who should have her for a wife would be very lucky."

Even disappointed suitors like Nick Biddle and Howard Cary wrote, "Your future wife is such as it is the privilege of few men to have." Alice Roosevelt wrote gushingly, "Oh, dearest Eleanor, it is simply too nice to be true." Eleanor had asked her to be one of her six bridesmaids.

Theodore Roosevelt, just after being re-elected, wrote Franklin, "We are greatly rejoiced over the good news. I am as fond of Eleanor as if she were my daughter; and I like you and trust you and believe in you . . . golden years open before you."

Eleanor wanted her uncle Teddy to give her away, but the wedding date must be planned around his busy schedule.

Since he was coming to New York on March 17th for St. Patrick's Day ceremonies, that would be an ideal time for the wedding.

Although he offered to have the ceremony "under his roof" and make all the arrangements for it, Eleanor had already accepted Cousin Susie's invitation to use the adjoining houses of hers and her mother's, Mrs. Ludlow, which could easily accommodate the two hundred guests invited.

Eleanor selected a wedding gown of heavy cream-colored satin trimmed with tulle and lace, with a long court train. Grandmother Hall offered her own Rosepoint Brussels lace veil, which Eleanor fastened with a diamond crescent pin that had been her mother's. She wore Sara's "dog collar" of pearls and carried a huge bouquet of lilies of the valley.

The house was decorated with lilacs, lilies of the valley, and pink rosebuds, the altar framed with palms and pink roses. The headmaster of Groton School, Dr. Endicott Peabody, would officiate. The bridesmaids wore cream taffeta with tulle veils and three feathers in their hair, reminders of the Roosevelt crest. Each of the ushers had tie pins Franklin had designed with three feathers in diamonds.

Franklin's mother wore black lace. She recorded in her journal, "Franklin is calm and happy. Eleanor the same."

The lapel watch which Franklin had given his bride had her initials outlined in diamonds. The pin to which it was fastened was designed with three feathers. sh e was, as she said, "decked out beyond description."

The wedding attracted much attention, not only because both the bride and groom were from socially prominent branches of the Roosevelt family, but because the President of the United States, a shamrock in his buttonhole, gave his niece away with a booming "I do."

When the ceremony was over, he kissed the bride, told

Franklin, "Glad you had sense enough to keep the name in the family," and strode away looking for refreshments. The crowd soon followed him, leaving the bride and groom alone. As Alice was heard to remark, "Father always wants to be the bride at every wedding and the corpse at every funeral."

They went directly from the wedding to Hyde Park, which Sara had turned over to them for their brief honeymoon. If Eleanor sensed Sara's subtlety in ordering their lives, she said nothing of that to Franklin, who accepted whatever his mother offered and may even have found it quite appropriate that he should bring his bride "home."

As Eleanor looked back at those early days of their marriage after thirty years, she wrote, "I marvel now at my husband's patience, for I realize how trying I must have been in many ways. I had an almost exaggerated idea of the necessity of keeping all of one's desires under complete subjugation. I can see today how funny were some of the tragedies of our early married life."

They lived in a small hotel in the West Forties while Franklin attended law school, and in the summer took an extended honeymoon trip to Europe. Both had been on the Grand Tour before, but it was different "poking into strange corners," as she wrote a friend, while Franklin looked for books and prints.

They traveled to Venice where Eleanor fed the birds on the Piazza San Marcos as she remembered doing as a little girl. They drifted over to Murano by gondola to see the glass blowers and ordered a set of glass with the Roosevelt crest as well as Venetian glass dolphins for table decorations.

Eleanor saw that they wrote to Mama frequently, telling her all the little details that would interest her. In Paris, Eleanor wrote, "Franklin got me some lovely furs . . . and of course I am delighted with them." She ordered linens and dresses, and since it was Sara's money that provided the trip, she was effusive in expressing affection: "You are always just the sweetest, dearest Mama to your children."

In the Dolomites Franklin wanted to climb a mountain, but Eleanor had never had any mountain climbing experience and panicked at the thought of the steep ascent. She learned that when Franklin had his mind set on something, he went ahead with it, finding an acquaintance there, Kitty Grandy, who owned a New York millinery shop, who said she'd be happy to climb with him.

Eleanor said nothing but reported later, "Though I never said a word, I was jealous beyond description and perfectly delighted when we started off again and drove out of the mountains."

They visited Franklin's aunt in Paris and friends in England and Scotland, one of whom asked Eleanor to explain the difference between the national and state governments in America. She couldn't do it, and it was Franklin who had to answer the question, speaking easily about states rights and the constitutional provisions for Federal authority. Embarrassed, Eleanor vowed when she returned home "to find out something about my own government."

They had asked Sara to find a house for them, and Eleanor looked forward to getting settled "with you to help us," she wrote her mother-in-law.

Eleanor had felt ill during the voyage home, with good reason. She was pregnant. They came back to New York to a house Sara Roosevelt had found for them a few blocks from her own. She had furnished it completely and engaged servants. There was nothing left for Eleanor to do but open the door. She had none of the worries of a young couple outfitting a new home, but none of the pleasures, either.

Furthermore, Sara supported them while Franklin was in

Eleanor and Franklin Roosevelt in Strathpeffer, Scotland during their 1905 honeymoon trip.

law school. Eleanor was acutely conscious of being dependent on Sara's generosity and considered it her duty to try to please Sara in every way. She went walking with her in the mornings, often driving on social rounds in the afternoon and usually having either luncheon or dinner with her mother-in-law.

The attention pleased Sara, for on Eleanor's twenty-first birthday Sara wrote her, hoping her "precious Franklin was making her happy, and blessing him for giving her such a dear, loving daughter."

It was fortunate that there were servants, for Eleanor had never been taught how to cook or manage a household. When baby Anna came in May, 1906, after a difficult and prolonged birth, Eleanor had no idea how to care for her. "I had never been interested in dolls or in little children, and I knew absolutely nothing about handling or feeding a baby." Sara found and engaged a nurse, and as other children came along, six in ten years, a succession of nurses took care of them.

During these ten years, Eleanor "was always just getting over having a baby or about to have one." James had a heart murmur and had to be carried up and down stairs. She had no life of her own but was just "absorbing the personalities of those around me." She was dominated by them, and her own activities seemed to be restricted to knitting, doing embroidery, or reading.

As the children kept coming, Sara built them a larger house and one for herself next door. There were double doors connecting the two drawing rooms and dining rooms, so Eleanor never knew when her mother-in-law might pop in "to be helpful." Although she relied on Sara for advice on everything from what to do about a fretful baby to how to arrange a dinner party, she had no privacy.

Once Franklin found her sobbing in front of her bedroom dressing table and asked what was the matter.

"I don't like living in a house which is not in any way mine. It does not represent how I want to live."

Franklin told her not to be such a goose, but she felt, "there was a good deal of truth in what I said."

When they went to Campobello that summer, they lived with Sara in her large house on the island. Because Franklin loved to sail, Eleanor conquered her fear of the water to go along with him. She even learned to fish, but she never really felt an affinity for the active, outdoor life. During foggy days and cool evenings, she would sit by the fire and read.

Back in New York Eleanor led a quiet life, pregnant again. The third baby they named Franklin, Jr. His nurse said he was big and beautiful and no trouble at all. They were at Hyde Park in the fall when all three children had the flu, baby Franklin more seriously ill than the others. The doctor said he was afraid his heart had been affected. On November 8, his breathing stopped. He was barely eight months old.

Eleanor felt guilty for not caring for the baby herself. "I felt he had been left too much to the nurse, I knew too little about him, and that in some way I must be to blame." She grieved over the cruelty of leaving her baby "out there in the cold graveyard." It was an unhappy winter for the family. As she said, "I made myself and all those around me most unhappy." Duty required she stifle her grief and present a serene face to her family. For months she did what was expected, mechanically, sorrowfully.

Ten months later another boy was born, weighing eleven pounds fourteen ounces. She named him Elliott, after her father.

Franklin decided to leave the law firm and run for the state legislature. He campaigned in a "fire-station automobile," with shiny lamps and handles, and when it broke down or the gasoline was being poured in, the farmers stood around to watch and hear him explain, not only how the car worked, but how he wanted to represent these local people. In a speech twenty years later he told how much he had learned. "Politics should be tested by considering whether or not they add or detract from the individual security and the right of happiness."

No one expected this young man to win, but Franklin did win, the first Democrat elected from the district in thirty-two years, and they moved to Elk Street in Albany. They found a three-storey brownstone house near Washington Park with

Eleanor with her mother-in-law, Sara Delano Roosevelt. The young wife often felt intimidated and dominated by the demanding older woman.

its huge trees and a lake where she could take the children for walks. It seemed palatial after their narrow New York house, with plenty of room for the children and their nurses. It even had a little garden.

Many senators commuted to Albany only when the legislature was in session, and when Albany society found that the handsome new legislator and his wife planned to live there, engraved invitations began to fill their mailbox.

Their own entertaining began immediately. It was fortunate that the house was large, for Franklin invited his constituents who had come up for the inauguration to a catered lunch. Franklin was fond of telling later that there were four hundred who came, including a band and the Hyde Park Fife and Drum Corps.

Franklin made their home the gathering place for politicians, particularly some who were against Boss rule. Sometimes Eleanor sat with them in the library and listened to their talk; often they joined her in the living room where she sat knitting or reading. She arranged frequent dinners and met many influential men, like Alfred E. Smith, majority leader of the assembly, and Robert Wagner, president *pro tem* of the Senate.

For the first time in their married life Eleanor was independent, the mistress of her own house with no relative to tell her what to do. High spirited Franklin liked the young, party-loving crowd, but Eleanor found them frivolous and shallow and preferred to stay home. She was more at ease with older friends.

But Eleanor believed it was a wife's duty to take an active interest in her husband's work. Occasionally she went to the gallery of the capitol to listen to speeches, admiring the marble walls and a balustrade of Sienna marble set off by red granite columns. There was a stained glass window above the dias, and there were carved oak beams that had obviously been there over a hundred years.

But Eleanor was home every afternoon to have tea with the three children. Everything she did was done out of a sense of duty, of what she ought to do. "I rarely thought of what I really wanted to do," she said.

Eleanor was "at home" every Wednesday for people to call on her, as was the custom. Sometimes when women from different countries came, she interpreted for them in three languages. She gave the necessary dinners to further Franklin's career, and gradually her shyness began to disappear. Soon others deferred to her judgment. Her natural curiosity, eagerness to learn, and a built-in thoughtfulness for others made her a popular hostess. She called on the wives of new legislators, and as a new venture, the wives of newspaper men.

One of these newspaper correspondents was Louis Howe, who was to become an important figure in the lives of both the Roosevelts. Elliott characterized him as "having more skills at his fingertips than half a dozen other men combined. He could write anything from a poem to a fast-breaking news story, and his . . . tireless research and astute political analysis . . . made him an uncannily accurate forecaster of election results."

He directed the campaign for Franklin's re-election, as Franklin was ill with typhoid fever at the time. Eleanor did not really like the man at first. She described him as "gnome-like, with a pock-marked face." He also alienated people by smoking several packs of cigarettes a day. But Franklin won the election.

He was not to serve long in a second term, however, for Josephus Daniels, Secretary of the Navy, asked Franklin to come to Washington as his assistant. When he accepted, he told Daniels, "All my life I have loved ships and have been a student of the Navy, and the Assistant Secretaryship is the one place, above all others, I would love to hold."

Eleanor was not consulted. "It never occurred to me," she reported, "to question where we were to go or what we were to do or how we were to do it." But she didn't look forward to life in Washington.

As Elliott wrote, "Mother was so painfully uncertain of herself that social life other than among her family and close friends was an ordeal. She could not rid herself of fear of the obligations it would place on her. But Father found enormous fun in meeting anybody."

Eleanor's shyness began to wear off through the necessity of meeting so many people. She had to call on the wives of all the officials and learned how to schedule between ten and thirty calls every afternoon and still be home for tea. "The children were always with me for an hour before their own supper and bedtime," she recorded.

Eleanor with the Roosevelts' first child, Anna, in 1906.

Franklin, Eleanor, and Anna Roosevelt with dog "Duffy" on vacation at Campobello, about 1907.

Franklin asked her to come with him on his first inspection trip to Mississippi, Florida, and Georgia. It was different scenery and a welcome change from Washington. She later went to various naval installations all over the country with no idea she was laying the foundations for far more important trips later.

Eleanor had two more babies during the Washington years. In August, 1914, with the war beginning in Europe, her fifth baby was born whom they also named Franklin, Jr., since the first Franklin, Jr. had died. A year and a half later, baby John arrived.

Life became more hectic after America declared war on Germany and her allies in April of 1917. Eleanor volunteered for work at the Union Station canteen, for the Navy League, the Navy Red Cross, the Navy Relief Society, and two days a week she visited the Naval Hospital. Everyone was doing "war work." Her brother Hall was working for the General Electric Company in Schenectady and soon enlisted in the air force. Eleanor and Franklin had their separate activities and saw little of each other.

To keep up with her social duties, Eleanor had engaged a social secretary, Lucy Page Mercer, whose family was well known but now poor. Her background enabled her to fit in well with the family, and Eleanor often asked her when she needed an extra woman at dinner parties. she seemed fond of both Eleanor and Franklin, and although Franklin called her "the lovely Lucy," Eleanor paid no attention at first as Franklin was apt to compliment all pretty women.

But when he insisted Eleanor take the children and spend the summer at Campobello, leaving Lucy in charge, she had some misgivings. Elliott later analyzed the situation. "With a mounting sense of insecurity, Mother continued to watch and wait, letting Father know in her own guarded way that her suspicions were beginning to harden."

Franklin wrote the day after the family departed, "You were a goosy girl to think . . . that I don't want you here all summer, because you know that I do . . . I am unreasonable and touchy now, but I shall try to improve."

But when Franklin developed a throat infection, Eleanor hurried home to nurse him. When he did come to Campobello for a few days, she wrote him as soon as he had left, "The chicks and I bemoaned our sad fate all through breakfast."

Later Franklin was sent on a naval inspection tour. He wrote her almost every day how much he missed her. When he was on his way home, the Navy Department called Eleanor to say that her husband was ill with pneumonia and she must have an ambulance with a stretcher waiting as the ship docked.

In pre-penicillin days, pneumonia could be a killer, and Eleanor soon had him settled in bed. When she unpacked his suitcase and put his things away in the bureau, she discovered something that drove out all thoughts of pneumonia and turned her world upside down.

Eleanor found some letters, unmistakably love letters, that Lucy Mercer had written to Franklin. Elliott says, "She had no compunction about reading them. They were the concrete evidence she had lacked and long waited for. She immediately called on Granny as an ally who would back her to the hilt. Mother would have preferred a divorce. That was her first thought and her first tactic was to offer it."

But Sara held rigid ideas about divorce and broken homes. If there was a divorce, she could cut off Franklin's money. Louis Howe told him divorce would be political suicide as he was already being talked about as Presidential material. Franklin agreed not to see Lucy again. The marriage would continue, although, Elliott points out, "their marital relations could never be resumed. She was willing to have him as a partner in public life, but not ever again as a husband."

Eleanor had been rejected for a younger, prettier woman. It was bound to be a turning point in her life. "I could forgive, but not forget," she confessed. She wrote in her diary the next year, "All my self-confidence is gone and I am on edge."

She stepped up the pace of her war work, managed her household, and went with Franklin when he accompanied

President Wilson to the Paris Peace Conference and brought back the charter of the League of Nations. Outwardly she seemed the same serene person, doing what was expected of her.

But Eleanor had put a distance between herself and Franklin that could not be bridged. She began to think of herself and what she wanted to do: learn to cook, for instance, to drive a car, perhaps even to go to business school to learn typing and shorthand. She would no longer be dependent on others, and if Franklin did not need her any longer, she would turn to people who did.

Louis Howe was one of these. He had influenced Franklin to run for Vice-President, and Louis Howe needed her help in the campaign. If she was to remain Franklin's wife, she must continue to give him her public support, Louis reminded her. Howe coached her in her behavior as a candidate's wife. He also saw her as a person, saying that she was intelligent, capable in many ways, sensitive, compassionate, with much to give. She could confide her fears to Louis and be sure of his understanding and help. Slowly her self-confidence grew.

On the campaign train, the *Westboro,* Eleanor stood beside her husband on the back platform, waving to the crowds, reaching down to shake an extended hand. Howe discussed Franklin's campaign speeches with her, asked for her opinion and seemed to value it. When Franklin and his aides played poker in the free evenings, Eleanor and Louis Howe found they could talk about everything from politics to feelings. Overlooking his strange appearance and incessant smoking, Eleanor had found a friend.

This was the first year, 1920, that women had been able to vote, but too many of them voted for Warren Harding and Calvin Coolidge instead of for Cox and Roosevelt, and the Democrats lost. Franklin joined the Fidelity and Trust

Company, a bonding firm, and told a fellow lawyer, Felix Frankfurter, later a justice of the Supreme Court, "I am delighted to get back into the real world again."

Howe pointed out to Eleanor the power of organizations to accomplish their ideals, and she became active in the League of Women Voters, the Women's Trade Union League, and the Women's Division of the New York State Democratic Party, working hard for causes they fostered. Here she met and became friends with several women, many of them already friends living in Greenwich Village: Marion Dickerman and Nancy Cook, a twosome active in the Democratic Party; Esther Lape and lawyer Elizabeth Reed of the League of Women Voters; and the socialist Rose Schneiderman, Director of the Women's Trade Union League.

These were very different from the debutante girls Eleanor had grown up with. They all had keen minds and were devoted to making the world a better place. And Eleanor, as she said later, "was thinking things out for myself and becoming an individual."

Since Eleanor was eager to work, the women soon recognized her leadership abilities. They enjoyed each other's company in a comradeship that was to last for many years. Eleanor spent one evening a week reading aloud with Esther and Elizabeth; another night she taught women workers how to read. These were the things that made life worth living and "added to my understanding of other human beings."

The love that had been repressed with Franklin's rejection Eleanor now began to lavish upon her friends in a different way. She was there when any of them needed her with her sympathy, understanding, and practical concern.

But Eleanor took time for the children's problems, too. Anna seemed uninterested in her school, which even her mother agreed was "stuffy." James needed good grades to qualify for Groton (which it was taken for granted all the boys would attend when they reached the age of twelve). Eleanor got up early that winter to hear his lessons before school. She scolded him for not caring to make use of any of his advantages. But lectures had little effect, and James continued to do better in football than in his academic classes.

Somehow Eleanor was more relaxed with "the babies," Franklin, Jr. and John. She took them for walks and arranged parties. Elliott, the middle one, tended to feel left out, often teased by James and Anna and appealing to his mother for protection. Perhaps because he bore her beloved father's name, Eleanor took special pains with Elliott, who seemed to need her more than the other children did.

The anxieties of bringing up her own children made Eleanor appreciate the problems her grandmother had had, and when Mrs. Hall died in 1919, Eleanor wrote in her diary, "It is only of late years that I have realized what it meant for her to take Hall, Ellie, and me into her home as she did."

To put together the pieces of the ruptured marriage, Eleanor kept the household account books as Franklin liked to have them done, and wrote to Sara, "I hope Franklin will be pleased." She bought some new clothes and noted that Franklin had liked her in the evening dress. When he went to hunt moose with Lieutenant Commander Richard E. Byrd, she wrote him, "I hated to have you go off alone and shan't feel quite happy till you are safely home again."

Eleanor slowly regained her confidence. Later she would write, "My experience has been that work is almost the best way to pull oneself out of the depths."

She needed all her resources to meet another crisis with Franklin at Campobello in 1921.

Chapter 3
Polio and What to do About It

Summer to the Roosevelts meant Campobello Island off the coast of Maine. Here Franklin had spent his boyhood summers learning to sail and beginning his lifelong interest in the sea and its ships. Sara Roosevelt had given Eleanor and Franklin a house next to her "cottage," and similar in its porches, wicker chairs, and hammocks ready for relaxing. On gray and foggy days, driftwood burned in the fireplaces took some of the dampness away.

Eleanor, the children, and servants were already enjoying the coolness and freedom of the island when Franklin sailed to Campobello on the yacht of a friend, Van-Lear Black. Elliott Roosevelt wrote later that "reaching Campobello by conventional means bored Father." New York to Boston by train took six hours. There were two more train changes until they reached the Eastport, Maine, station, then a carriage ride to the sardine docks where a motorboat waited to cross two miles of sea to the island.

The children could hardly wait for Franklin to arrive. Elliott says, too, "It was dull without Father." Eleanor read aloud every evening by the fire, they could swim and go on picnics, but Franklin was the fun-loving, joking parent while Eleanor was the organizer and disciplinarian.

The day after Franklin arrived, he took Van-Lear Black out fishing. On the slippery deck Franklin lost his balance and toppled over the side into the icy waters of the Bay of Fundy. He thought nothing of it at the time, although it did give him a slight chill.

The next day he took the whole family on a picnic, and

on the way home they noticed a brush fire had started. When they had beaten out the flames with freshly cut evergreen boughs, Franklin led them at a dog-trot two miles across the island to a freshwater lake for a swim, and then for a quick dip into the freezing waters of Herring Cove.

When they reached home, Eleanor sent the shivering children to change into warm clothes, but the mail had come and Franklin, as he said later, "sat reading for a while, too tired even to dress. I'd never felt quite that way before." He felt a chill and said he was going to bed to get warm. He didn't want to catch cold and spoil the fun.

The next morning he could hardly get out of bed and his temperature was 102. Eleanor sent for Dr. Bennett, who said he thought it was just a cold. Eleanor and Louis Howe, who was visiting with his wife and son, were not convinced. They had planned a three-day camping trip and decided to send the children off with Grace Howe.

Eleanor called the doctor again the following day when Franklin could not stand up. The pain in his back and legs turned to numbness and a weakness in his whole body. Howe went to Eastport with the doctor to try to locate a specialist and found a Dr. Keen vacationing in Bar Harbor, a hundred miles down the coast, who agreed to come.

Eleanor had moved a cot into Franklin's bedroom and discovered her husband was completely paralyzed. The renowned specialist diagnosed the problem as a blood clot on the spine, recommended massage, and said the condition would clear up in time.

Eleanor and Louis Howe took turns massaging Franklin's twisted legs and feet, bathing him, lifting and turning him, every movement bringing torturous pain. Yet when the children came to the door, he managed a reassuring grin and never complained.

Uncle Fred Delano, to whom both Louis and Eleanor had

42

written describing Franklin's symptoms, consulted a specialist in Boston who, without seeing the patient, correctly diagnosed the disease as polio and said to stop the massage, as it was dangerous to begin it that soon. Eleanor called a Boston specialist in polio, Dr. Robert Lovett, who confirmed the long-distance diagnosis. He felt that the overexertion and chilling had increased the severity of the attack and that the massage had damaged muscle tissue. But he praised the nursing skills of both Eleanor and Howe and prescribed hot baths to soothe the patient's pain.

Dr. Keen suggested Eleanor get a trained nurse. He wrote to her, "You have been a rare wife and have borne your heavy burden most bravely. You will surely break down if you do not have immediate relief."

So a Miss Rocky was brought up from New York, and after she arrived Howe returned to New York to handle Franklin's business affairs. He and Eleanor had agreed that the outside world should not know the extent of Franklin's illness. He said only that Franklin had had a chill and fever and should return by the middle of the next month.

Sara Roosevelt had been in Europe, and Eleanor asked Franklin's half brother, Rosy, to meet her when the ship docked in New York and explain that Franklin was ill and couldn't be there. The next day she arrived at Campobello. Franklin was paralyzed from the chest down but was still hearty and cheerful, saying to his mother, "Well, I'm glad you are back, Mama, and I got up this party for you."

It was several weeks before Franklin was ready for the journey home. Uncle Fred supplied a private railroad car, but Louis Howe organized the ordeal of lowering the helpless patient in a sling down the front steps, onto a stretcher, down a steep path to the waiting motorboat, and on shore to shove the stretcher through an open window of the compartment on the train.

At Grand Central a report for the New York *World* wrote, "Mr. Roosevelt was enjoying his cigarette and said he had a good appetite. Although unable to sit up, he says he is feeling more comfortable." Two days later, after he had been moved to Presbyterian Hospital, Howe broke the story to the newspapers that Franklin had poliomyelitis, but that his doctor said, "He will not be crippled. No one need have any fear of permanent injury from this attack."

He did not go home to Sixty-fifth Street until early in November. But before this move Eleanor fought and won her most decisive battle with her mother-in-law. Sara, who always considered she knew what was best for her son, wanted Franklin to come home to Hyde Park. She was convinced he would be a helpless invalid the rest of his life, and she wanted him with her where she could give him every comfort.

Eleanor sensed that Franklin, at thirty-nine, would be unhappy in a life of idleness. There was nothing the matter with his brain, and she agreed with Louis Howe that the best hope for Franklin's recovery was to keep up his interest in politics. She could see him directing efforts toward social improvements and promoting some of the reforms she had become interested in.

There were many arguments with the dictatorial Sara, and "discussions about his care became acrimonious at times," she recalled. Sara thought the people Eleanor brought to see Franklin sapped his vitality, while Eleanor saw that keeping up his business and political interests helped to strengthen Franklin's conviction that he would soon be well again.

He was often in pain. His legs had to be placed in plaster casts to stretch the tendons behind each knee into a straight position again. And Sara was right next door to come over daily and renew her arguments that what Franklin needed was rest.

Eleanor only broke down once. She was reading to the boys, eleven and five years old, when she suddenly began to cry and couldn't stop. There was no place in the house where Eleanor could have hysterics in private. She slept on a cot in one of the boys' rooms; she had given Louis Howe Anna's room, the nurse had another. "I dressed in my husband's bathroom," she said. "In the daytime I was too busy to need a room."

And Anna was unhappy. She thought it unfair (could it have been Sara's subtle suggestion?) that Louis Howe should have her room and she should be shunted off to a little fourth-floor room.

All the tensions of Franklin's illness, Sara's constant nagging, and Anna's fifteen-year-old's outbursts had been building inside until they spilled over in wrenching sobs.

Eleanor went through into Sara's house, as she had moved to the country, found a vacant room, locked the door and stayed there for two hours. "Eventually," she wrote later, "I pulled myself together . . . this is the one and only time I remember in my entire life having gone to pieces in this particular manner. From that time on I seem to have got rid of nerves and uncontrollable tears."

But Eleanor looked back on that year as "in many ways the most trying winter of my entire life." And yet she emerged victorious in the battle with Sara. If she had not, she later said, she would have become "a completely colorless echo of my husband and mother-in-law and torn between them, I might have stayed a weak character forever if I had not found that out."

Louis Howe urged Eleanor to become more active in political life herself. She had never done anything on her own for a political organization, nor had she ever made a speech before a large audience. But she presided at a luncheon to raise funds for the women's division of the Democratic State Committee; she drove people to the polls on election day; she started a paper for the Committee and learned from Louis Howe "a great deal about advertising, circulation, and make-up . . . and how to make a dummy for the printer."

Louis Howe also gave her valuable help on the speeches she was called upon to make. "I had a bad habit, because I was nervous," she wrote, "of laughing when there was nothing to laugh at. He broke me of that by showing me how inane it sounded. His advice was, Have something you want to say, say it, and sit down.'"

Meanwhile, Franklin was struggling with his disability. He learned to use crutches and could walk with them a little way every day. He had a trapeze over his bed where he could exercise his arms and upper body. He tried to swim by crawling up to the edge of the water and sliding in. But he needed someone standing by to pull him out.

If he dropped something that fell out of his reach, he had to wait until someone else picked it up for him. Finally he had a carpenter make him a pair of pincers on a long stick. He began crawling on the floor, pulling his legs after him, so that in case of fire he would not be trapped.

Through it all Franklin remained cheerful, and although he had times of depression when he questioned whether he would ever again be well, he kept his sense of humor, played on the floor with the boys until they forgot he could not get up by himself, spent hours on his stamp collection, and joked with visitors.

By February, steel braces, each weighing seven pounds, were fitted to his legs from hip to ankle. He learned to push himself up by his arms from the wheelchair, reach for his crutches, and walk until he couldn't take another step. He was determined that some day he would discard both braces and crutches forever.

When someone asked Eleanor years later how she felt about her husband's illness, she answered, "I do not think I ever stopped to analyze my feelings. There was so much to do to manage the household and the children and to try to keep things running smoothly that I never had any time to think of my own reactions. I simply lived from day to day and got through them the best I could."

Franklin and a friend bought a boat together, a "barge," Elliott called it. Franklin had looked for one "that is fairly low in the water so that I can easily drop overboard and crawl back on deck. Also, if possible, a boat whose cabin is not down a ladder."

He cruised off the coast of Florida in the winter time, always with guests and his secretary, Missy LeHand, who handled the mail, wrote his letters to keep in touch with political and business associates, and joined him in fishing and swimming excursions. She reported that "there were days when it was noon before he could pull himself out of depression and greet his guests wearing his light-hearted face."

Eleanor stayed in New York and wrote Franklin about the bills. "I find after paying all the household bills up to date and cash for food . . . I have $151.16. . . . Please send me what you can . . . but in any case be sure to send me the house $1000 so I will get it on the 1st."

Franklin's salary from the Fidelity company continued at $25,000 a year, but with his hospital costs, the ongoing household expenses, and those of maintaining the boat, its captain and cook and succession of guests, Eleanor had to dip into her meager trust fund, and Franklin sold some of his naval prints and ship models at auction to raise $4,537.

They went to Hyde Park for the summers, where Sara

47

had had an elevator installed and ramps on some of the steps. Eleanor encouraged Franklin when he felt sure complete recovery was possible, but everything he tried seemed to fail: massage, saltwater baths, ultraviolet light, electrical current shocks, and experiments in walking.

He did his exercises in the morning and made his walking sessions entertaining to anyone watching. He liked having people around to applaud his efforts and did not like being alone. He turned each session into a learning situation for the children, explaining how each muscle worked. He invited them to feel how strong his arm muscles were. After his braces were on, he grabbed at the parallel bars, waist high, and said, "See how easily I can walk now." Or he'd have the parallel bars mounted above his head, and hanging from them, he'd propel his legs along until he seemed to be walking.

Louis Howe was there every day working with or entertaining Franklin with his hobby of making model boats. Sometimes they would catalogue stamps or record birds they had seen. Sara only tolerated him during the day because Franklin wanted him. She never invited him to spend the night. Calling him "that dirty little man," Sara made no secret of her dislike of Howe.

Eleanor, however, appreciated his concern for her husband and also for her. When she had to give a speech, Louis offered to write it for her. Then he would listen attentively as she practiced delivering it and give her suggestions for improving her delivery.

In the 1922 Democratic Convention in Syracuse, Eleanor played a major part. She rallied all the Dutchess County delegates to vote for Al Smith's nomination for governor. She had given a picnic at Hyde Park for the wives of forty mayors in upstate New York, and she held a reception for the members of Odd Fellows and Rebeccas. She had always been happiest when she felt useful, and so "I was eager to do what I could."

Eleanor even went with Howe and Henry Morgenthau, their neighbor and influential friend, to Syracuse. When Smith was nominated by a large majority, he wrote Franklin, "I had quite a session with our lady politicians, as Mrs. Roosevelt no doubt told you. I was delighted to see her taking an active part, and I am really sorry that you could not be there. But take care of yourself—there is another day coming."

That day came two years later when Smith decided to run for re-election. By this time Eleanor had become a major influence in the Women's Division of the Democratic State Committee. She, with Nancy Cook and Marion Dickerman, had organized all but five counties of the state by the spring of 1924 and succeeded in getting women delegates selected by women.

Franklin came from Warm Springs to nominate Smith, and Eleanor seconded the nomination.

Franklin had purchased the run-down resort in Georgia from George Foster Peabody, a New York banker. When he had visited the springs, he felt "the water does my legs more good than anything else." Eleanor was afraid they could not afford the venture. She felt they needed the money to educate the children. "Don't let yourself in for too much money," she warned. "One cannot have vital interests in widely divided places."

But Franklin liked the place and the people and wanted to own it. Eleanor went there as seldom as possible. Poverty in the area eighty miles south of Atlanta and ten miles from the nearest paved road "made me sad, and the southern prejudice against Blacks made me angry." But if Franklin felt the baths helped, she accepted his word, particularly when an article in the Atlanta *Journal* reported that Franklin "was literally swimming himself back to health and strength."

Anna married Curtis Dall, and in March, 1927, Eleanor's first grandchild was born. Sara wrote Franklin she was sorry he couldn't have been there. "Eleanor sat all night with Anna and came to my room this morning perfectly dressed and her hair perfect as if she had just left the dinner table. I think she is a wonder."

Sara could praise one moment, however, and annoy the next. Eleanor wrote Franklin, "Mama has done nothing but get in little side slaps today." And "Mama was awful last Sunday and made us feel each in turn that we'd like to chew her up." She could criticize Eleanor unmercifully one day and then call her "a wonder, so busy and so sweet and so amiable all the time."

When Eleanor wrote Franklin that "she couldn't stand" staying at Hyde Park with Mama any longer, he suggested she and her friends build a get-away cottage a few miles away. She was to mark out the land she wanted and he would get someone to supervise the project. So a fieldstone cottage was built on the Val-Kill stream, and that dammed up to create a lake where Franklin could come to swim.

Nancy Cook built some of the furniture for the cottage, and that grew into the establishment of a furniture factory on the premises with the idea of giving employment to local boys wanting to learn a trade. Their first project was to build furniture for Franklin's new cottage he had had built at Warm Springs. At their first exhibition in 1927 the *New York Times* said, "The work is handwrought and beautifully finished in every detail and copied with exactness from genuine antiques."

Eleanor joined with Nancy in buying the private school where she taught. Here Eleanor taught English, drama, and American literature. As Mlle.Souvestre had done, Eleanor taught the girls to think for themselves and took them to settlement houses, tenements, and police line-ups so they could have a broader perspective on city governments and social problems. She emphasized "the connection between things of the past and things of today."

But Eleanor never gave up her interest in politics, particularly when in 1928 Al Smith decided to make a try for the Presidency. Though some thought him uneducated, uncouth, he had brought about many social reforms in New York State, and the Democrats rallied to the defense of "the man of the people."

Smith asked Franklin to place his name in nomination. And Franklin agreed.

But he refused to appear in public in a wheelchair. He announced that he would do it alone, with braces and two canes. He was determined to prove that he was not a helpless cripple, that he could still merit the confidence of the people.

It was slow progress to the podium at the convention, and Eleanor joined in the spontaneous, prolonged applause when Franklin made it, threw back his head, and flashed his famous smile. His speech was later rated one of the great political speeches of all time, and the applause following it lasted for an hour and fifteen minutes.

Smith, sure that he would win the Presidency, convinced Franklin that he should run for the governorship Smith was leaving. Eleanor was too busy working behind the scenes at the national office to go out on the campaign trail, but Franklin campaigned vigorously throughout the state.

Once when he had made speeches in Herkimer, Fonda, Amsterdam, Gloversville, Schenectady, and Troy in one day, he quipped, "Too bad about this unfortunate sick man, isn't it?" He rode in an open touring car with a steel bar on the back of the front seat. Here he could pull himself up to a standing position by snapping his braces locked.

Late on the night of the election when he and Eleanor left state headquarters, the outcome was still uncertain. But the next morning when the final figures were in, Franklin was governor-elect by a very narrow margin.

Al Smith lost the election to Herbert Hoover. He had seen the governorship of the state of New York as a stepping stone to the Presidency, as it had been for Theodore Roosevelt. It didn't work that way for Smith, but it paved the way for his successor.

Franklin was again in a position of power. It was the first time a severely paralyzed man had ever been elected to public office.

Those who knew about his struggles saw it as a tribute to his courage and perseverance. Others might see it as a triumph for Eleanor's and Louis Howe's patient persistence and encouragement.

Chapter 4
Wife of a Governor and a President

The Albany years, as Eleanor wrote later, "cast their shadow before them." As Governor, Franklin could try out some of the ideas he would later initiate as President.

Eleanor had not been as thrilled as the reporters thought the Governor-elect's wife should be. "No," she had said, "I am not excited about my husband's election. I don't care. What difference can it make to me?" In fact, she had been fearful that she would have to give up much of her newly found independence and become again merely the figurehead wife, presiding at dinners and teas and having no part on the political scene she had come to enjoy.

But Franklin's office was not at the Capitol but in the Executive Mansion, a large, brick-red building with Victorian cupolas. The room Smith had used as his office she made over into a family sitting room and workroom for herself. She wanted to keep on teaching, and so was in New York from Monday to Wednesday noon, and in Albany for the rest of the week. She served tea every afternoon, often with chocolate cake, including guests, secretaries, friends, anyone she happened to meet and invite. There were nine guest rooms in the Mansion, usually full. Both Franklin and Eleanor enjoyed people.

On Sundays before she left, Eleanor had a list of all guests who would be staying there while she was away and left precise instructions with the major-domo for room assignments, seating arrangements, menus, and other details. On the train to New York, she made out lesson plans, corrected papers, and wrote notes on the answers to letters she would dictate to Miss Thompson when she got to New York.

Eleanor was especially interested in seeing that more women came into government and made sure Franklin knew her views. But she was careful how she phrased her suggestions to Franklin, for he had made it clear to Al Smith, who wanted to retain his influence in New York State politics, that the new governor would make his own decisions. He had replaced Smith appointees with his own people. "I hope you will consider making Frances Perkins Labor Commissioner," Eleanor wrote to Franklin when he was at Warm Springs before assuming the governorship. And "Don't let Mrs. M. get draped around you for she means to be." Mrs. Moskowitz had been a power in Smith's ruling group, and Franklin took Eleanor's warning into consideration when he selected his staff. Mrs. M. was out.

Frances Perkins was in, as was Harry Hopkins managing the relief and welfare departments, and Henry Morgenthau, Jr., a neighbor at Hyde Park, as Conservation Commissioner, all willing to try new programs. "It was part of Franklin's political philosophy," Eleanor said, "that the greata benefit to be derived from having forty-eight states was the possibility of experimenting in a small scale to see how a program worked before trying it out nationally."

Eleanor and Franklin both shared an interest in education, social reform, and relief and general welfare. Franklin was also committed to improvements in soil conservation, forestry, the development of water power, in the Indian conflict, and transportation problems generally.

The State of New York had a boat available for State officials to travel on the Erie Canal, and Franklin decided to use this on an inspection trip. He asked Eleanor's help in analyzing conditions inside prisons, state hospitals, and other installations, since it would have been too difficult for him to walk through the buildings. At first Eleanor reported what she had seen, but Franklin wanted to know more for ammunition when he met with the legislative appropriations committee later on. So Eleanor reported, "I learned to look into the cooking pots on the stove to find out if the contents corresponded to the menu; I learned to notice whether the beds were too close together. . . to watch the patients' attitude toward the staff, and before the end of our years in Albany, I had become a fairly expert reporter on state institutions."

Sergeant Earl Miller, a state trooper assigned to the governor's detail, also was delegated by Franklin to accompany Eleanor when she went out alone. Earl gave her additional tips in appraising a state institution. He suggested she arrive unannounced to get a true picture, which she began to do on other trips.

Earl, a handsome young man, was a fine horseman who did trick riding at the state fair. He gave Eleanor riding lessons, and before she went to Washington, a horse of her own named Dot. Eleanor found out he had been a circus acrobat, had served in the Navy, and had had an unhappy first marriage. Eleanor's ready sympathies were aroused, and she grew as fond of Earl as she would one of her son's friends.

Of course the gossips made much of her friendship with Earl, hinting that they were having an affair. But Eleanor was heard to remark to a friend, "You don't sleep with someone who calls you 'Mrs. Roosevelt.'" She went her serene way, enjoying Earl's company, mothering him, and accepting his counsel much as she did Louis Howe's. When he decided to marry again, the wedding took place at Hyde Park.

As chairman of the Finance Committee of the Women's Trade Union, Eleanor and her group had raised enough money to pay off the mortgage on their clubhouse. And when the organization's twenty-fifth anniversary approached, Sara Roosevelt invited them to have a celebration party at Hyde Park. They chartered a bus so that shop girls and trade union officials could travel to the party. Eleanor made sure that the governor put in an appearance, reminding him "You are the *piece de resistance.*"

One of Eleanor's colleagues wrote to him afterwards, "You were the main topic of conversation all the way down the river. The girls were saying over and over again, 'was not the Governor great?', what a kind face he has, and how democratic he is, etc. . . . I wish there were a million more like you and Eleanor."

People sensed Eleanor's ready sympathy and wrote her about their problems. Mothers inquired about their sons in mental institutions or in jail, and she answered each letter, often forwarding the petitions to those who might be able to do something about the situation.

After the stock market crash in 1929, these rivers of appeals became a torrent. Sometimes Eleanor showed these letters to Franklin, asking, "How shall I answer or will you?" She advised her petitioners not to come to New York looking for work. "At the present time there are countless numbers of people out of employment here and I am not able to get positions for any one." But she tried.

When Franklin decided to run for a second term in 1930, Eleanor, together with the women's division of the Democratic Party, went in to action behind the scenes, organizing meetings, planning strategy, and writing editorials in the *Democratic News.*

As the campaign drew to a climax, Eleanor told an interviewer, "If my husband is reelected, I shall be pleased. And if he isn't, well, the world is full of interesting things to do."

Franklin was reelected by a landslide. There was a victory celebration at Hyde Park. Eleanor had to leave early for New York so she wrote a good-night note to her husband, "Much love and a world of congratulations. It is a triumph in so many ways, dear, and so well earned. Bless you and good luck these next two years. E. R."

Eleanor had told an interviewer about the ideal type of modern wife who must be partner, mother, homemaker, and in that order. "Everything else depends upon the success of the wife and husband in their personal relationship," she said. At this stage of their lives she tried for more companionship with Franklin, a real partnership of equals based on an affection that did not die with rejected love.

But Franklin and Louis Hose had set their sights on the Presidency, and Franklin became more and more occupied with political problems and had less time for talk of personal matters with Eleanor. He had no trouble being reelected for a second term as governor, and that decisive victory kept his name before the public.

The night of the nominating convention they listened to the speeches in Albany. The balloting did not begin until 4:30 A.M. Eleanor sent pots of coffee out to the newsmen and knitted a sweater for Louis Howe who, though ill with asthma, was at the Chicago convention. The convention finally recessed at 9:30 A.M. without the necessary votes for a nomination, and it was not until dinner that night that the behind-stage politicking of Louis Howe, Jim Farley, and others brought about the nomination of Franklin Delano Roosevelt.

The newspaper people, including Lorena Hickok, who was to become Eleanor's close friend, had had no dinner, and as Eleanor said, "nothing to eat except the eggs I had cooked for them in the middle of the night." She invited them all to have breakfast with her on the porch.

Two days later Franklin and Eleanor, with John and Elliott, the secretaries, Missy LeHand and Grace Tully, and Franklin's two bodyguards, Earl Miller and Gus Gennerich, flew to Chicago where Franklin made his acceptance speech. Flying to a convention was something no candidate had done before, and Elliott reported it a rough trip with stops for fuel in Buffalo and Cleveland and a descent through a rain squall.

But Franklin's speech fulfilled its purpose, which was to draw the country together in the effort to restore prosperity. He ended with words that became a slogan for his Presidency: "I pledge you, I pledge myself to a new deal for the American People. . . . Give me your help . . . to win in this crusade to restore America to its people."

Franklin traveled 13,000 miles before the election, but as Eleanor recalled, "I did not work directly in the campaign because I felt that that was something better done by others, but I went on many of the trips and always did anything that Franklin felt would be helpful."

Franklin came home from campaign trips "with a conviction that the Depression could be licked." He observed from the train window soil erosion, wastefulness, but he also sensed "a vitality in the people that could be salvaged." I believe it was from his faith in the people that he drew the words of his first inaugural address: "The only thing we have to fear is fear itself," Eleanor wrote later.

Eleanor had continued writing magazine articles, making radio speeches and teaching until a newspaper suggested that "as a matter of propriety and in keeping with the dignity of the exalted position her husband is about to hold, she ought to abandon some of her present occupations." Eleanor gave them all up, though she confessed she was afraid she'd be a prisoner in the White House "with nothing to do except stand in line and receive visitors and preside over official dinners."

She soon made being First Lady her own unique full-time job.

With Eleanor's independence and her desire to get things done quickly and efficiently, Eleanor shocked White House staff members by running the elevator herself and by moving furniture around without waiting for someone to help her. Each morning she must see, first the housekeeper with her menus for the day, then the head usher to check on the names of expected guests and family plans for coming and going, and finally her social secretary with lists of invitations, necessary receptions, teas which Eleanor thought "utterly futile and meaningless."

Miss Thompson (Tommy) then came in to start work on the mail. From March to December in 1933, Eleanor herself received 301,000 pieces of mail, all of which had to be answered and some requests investigated.

When the veterans returned to Washington to present their grievances, Eleanor urged her husband to see that they were adequately housed and fed and visited them herself. She had been appalled the previous summer when then-President Hoover had used military force to drive the veterans out of their shacks in Washington. One veteran, amid cheers of the others, said, "Hoover sent the army; Roosevelt sent his wife." And soon after they dispersed.

Eleanor came to feel that the White House symbolized the government, "and though standing and shaking hands for an hour or so, two or three times a week, is not exactly an inspiring occupation, still I think it well worth while. I did it regularly, three times a week during the winter months."

A glance at her social calendar for a week showed a daily luncheon for various groups, teas at 4 and at 5 P.M. every day but Friday, and a dinner for 22, a judicial reception, a diplomatic dinner for 94 with 197 additional guests for music after dinner.

Eleanor in 1933, the year Franklin began his first term as President of the United States.

In addition, Lorena Hickok suggested she hold press conferences for women journalists, an innovation for a First Lady. Eleanor admitted she was terrified at this new venture and wondered "whether I could handle press conferences without getting myself and him into trouble. Louis Howe and my husband alone seemed unworried." But later she could evaluate her meetings with the women of the press as "one of the most rewarding experiences of my White House life. Out of them I gained some friends whom I value very highly."

To impress women and the public at large of the safety and convenience of air travel, Eleanor flew to Baltimore with Amelia Earhart and a little later took her first transcontinental flight to Los Angeles. In those days it was a real event, and Will Rogers wrote in the *New York Times*, "It was a real boost for aviation, but here is what she takes a medal for: out at every stop, day or night, standing for photographs by the hour, being interviewed, talking over the radio, no sleep. And yet they say she never showed one sign of weariness or annoyance of any kind."

Even when Eleanor took a vacation, she had trained herself to be observant of conditions Franklin should know about. In Maine she learned about the life of a fisherman, what the farms were like, what type of education was available. She investigated the coal mining regions of West Virginia where she found men who had been on relief for years and children "who did not know what it was to sit down to a table and eat a proper meal."

Eleanor got influential people like Bernard Baruch to help establish a homestead project near Morgantown, and for several years she continued to visit the people. One woman compared last Christmas when they had had only carrots to chew on to this year with their own chicken and a toy for the children.

Economic recovery was the new President's chief concern. His "New Deal" resulted in various government agencies. Harry Hopkins was Federal Emergency Relief Administrator; the Civil Works Administration put four million people to work within a month; and the WPA

(Works Progress Administration) made work for the unemployed, as did the CCC (Civilian Conservation Corps). Eleanor took a personal interest in all these efforts and even drew praise from Westbrook Pegler. He later became one of Eleanor's chief critics, but at the time he wrote that nobody wasted time on useless formalities at the White House and "Mrs. Roosevelt has been busy on such undignified trivialities as old age pensions, a ban on child labor, and the protection of health of mothers and children."

In her travels around the country Eleanor saw the results of work done by the government agencies. "Soil conservation and forestry work went forward, recreation areas were built, and innumerable bridges, schools, hospitals and sanitation projects were constructed—lasting monuments to the good work done under these agencies," Eleanor wrote.

In 1934 Franklin suggested Eleanor make a trip to Puerto Rico where the sugar workers practically starved in off-seasons. She found little girls embroidering handkerchiefs for a few pennies, shacks with no sanitation, a lack of industries. "On my return," she said, "I begged my husband to send down some labor people and industrialists to develop new industries." This eventually was done.

Also in 1934, she resumed her radio talks, donating the money to the American Friends Service Committee in order to forestall the criticism she had experienced when she gave it up two years before. She became one of the highest paid radio personalities of the time, though as she said to a critic, "I think that you are entirely right, that no one is worth $500 a minute. Certainly I never dreamed for a minute I was!"

Just before the re-election campaign of 1936, Louis Howe became more seriously ill and moved from the White House to a hospital where he died. Louis' death was a great loss to Franklin. As Eleanor realized, "Louis' death deprived my husband of a close relationship and the satisfaction of having someone near to whom he could talk quite frankly." His funeral was conducted from the White House as if he had, in actuality, been a member of the First Family.

The term ended with the feeling, Eleanor thought, "that on the whole the country was getting back on its feet." She had played a part in making that possible. But could it last?

Chapter 5
Youth, Loyalty, Preparedness

The year 1936 was a watershed, a dividing point. The public began to feel that the Depression was behind them. More people were working, and they looked at the one percent deducted from their paychecks for the new Social Security plan as an investment that would eventually be returned to them as a pension.

There was no doubt that Franklin would run for a second term, and he won in a landslide election. By this time Eleanor and Lorena Hickok had become such close friends that they wrote frequent letters expressing deep affection and confiding inner thoughts they could share with no one else. Eleanor wrote in one letter, "I realize more and more that FDR is a great man, and he is nice to me, but as a person I'm a stranger, and I don't want to be anything else."

And yet when Franklin was away—he took a month's cruise to South America following the election—he signed his letters "loads and loads of love." At a stop in Trinidad, when he had word of King Edward's abdication, he wrote, "Do I or do I not propose the health of the king? Ever so much love. I've missed you and it will be good to be back."

Eleanor had decided to write her autobiography which she called "This is My Story." Her objectives were "to give a picture, if possible, of the world in which I grew up and which today is changed in so many ways, and to give as truthful a picture as possible of a human being. The more the world speeds up, the more it seems necessary that we should learn to pick out of the past the things that we feel were more important and beautiful then . . . the vanishing world in which I grew up, the influences and the values that dominated that era."

She had to work on the book whenever she could snatch the time. She had two other writing assignments with deadlines: a daily column syndicated in newspapers called "My Day," which must be in by six o'clock every evening, and a monthly column for the "Woman's Home Companion" magazine.

Eleanor never lacked material for these articles, for her days were full. She had all her continuing White House duties, and she also went on lecture tours. As she wrote to a friend, "It would be easier to be either the President's wife or the paid lecturer, but the combination is exhausting." She gave most of the money she earned to various charities.

One of these was the American Youth Congress. When she pointed out to Franklin that these out-of-school and out-of-work young people would soon be voters, Franklin instituted the National Youth Administration and allocated fifty million dollars to the program. Harry Hopkins said they might be criticized for regimenting youth the way Germany had, but Franklin answered, as Eleanor recalled, "If it's the right thing to be done, then it should be done. I guess we can stand the criticism."

They were both used to critical attacks, but Eleanor's response was to ignore them and continue her efforts to help causes she felt were important. And to her, nothing deserved her attention more at the time than to assist young people in getting jobs.

But there was a radical element in the organization which gradually assumed more power. Eleanor tried to advise the leaders to take a more rational approach if they wanted Congress to appropriate funds. She made personal friends of several, including young Joe Lash who would later write several books about Eleanor and Franklin. The best

Eleanor casts her vote--no doubt for husband Franklin--on Election Day in 1936, at Hyde Park.

leaders were earnest, sincere, full of hope. She wrote to him, "As time goes, I've known you a very short time, but I have a real sense of kinship and understanding, and I'd like you to feel you had a right to my love and that my home was always yours when you needed it or anything else which I have. . . My dear love to you."

When 4000 members of the Youth Congress came on a pilgrimage to Washington, Eleanor asked Franklin to speak to them. She put on a raincoat and joined them while the President spoke from the South Portico of the White House.

He was distressed about the Communist element in the group and lectured them about Russia being run by a dictatorship, and that as Americans he told them "you have no American right by act or deed of any kind, to subvert the government and Constitution of this nation."

The response of some was to boo him. Eleanor deplored such discourtesy and invited a few of the leaders to tea on Sunday afternoon. She expected to persuade the smaller group to have more patience, but when they, too, shouted down the President, accusing him of being responsible for mass unemployment, Eleanor spoke with her customary dignity and authority. "The President of the United States should not be insulted in such a disgraceful fashion." She was booed, too.

Eleanor knew there was a group trying to keep the communist element in check, and she allied herself with them and for a few more months helped them raise funds. she said afterward that she had not lost faith in youth, but only in the radical approach to solving problems. It had also, she said, given her an insight into Communist tactics which was useful to her in later political situations.

The Nazi-Soviet pact of August 21, 1939, completed the disillusionment that Joe Lash and other Youth Congress leaders felt, and he agreed with Eleanor that "Communism succeeds only as we ourselves fail."

To bolster ties with potential allies in case Mussolini's conquest of Ethiopia and Hitler's rantings about conquering the world should lead to war, various monarchs visited Washington. First came the Swedish crown prince and princess, then those from Denmark and Norway, and finally King George and Queen Elizabeth of Great Britain.

There were many matters of protocol to be decided. The king was supposed to be served thirty seconds before the queen. But what about the President and his wife? Franklin decided that he and the king should be served first, then the queen and Eleanor. The queen would sit on Franklin's right and the king on Eleanor's right.

In her column and later in the second volume of her autobiography, Eleanor gave a full account of the arrival of Their Majesties at the train station, the parade through the Guard of Honor and the slow drive to the White House, Franklin and King George in one car, and Queen Elizabeth and Eleanor in another. Eleanor was fascinated watching the queen. "She had the most gracious manner and bowed right and left with interest, actually looking at people in the crowd so that I am sure many of them felt that her bow was really for them."

After lunch they drove around Washington, and Eleanor reported that the queen "endeared herself to me by saying suddenly, ' I saw in the paper that you were being attacked for having gone to a meeting of the WPA workers. It surprises me that there should be any criticism, for it is so much better to allow people with grievances to air them; and it is particularly valuable if they can do so to someone in whom they feel a sense of sympathy and who may be able to reach the head of the government with their grievances'."

There were garden parties, dinners and entertainments, visits to the Capitol, to Mt. Vernon where the king laid a wreath on Washington's tomb, to Arlington National Cemetery for a repeat at the tomb of the Unknown Soldiers and to a CCC camp where both the king and queen asked questions of the boys because the king wanted to set up something similar in Great Britain.

Presidential aide Harry Hopkins and his daughter Diana, aged eight, were living in the White House, and Diana wanted to see the queen. When Queen Elizabeth heard, she suggested Diana be in the hall as she and the king left for dinner at the British Embassy. When Eleanor presented

Diana, she curtsied to the regal figure in a white, spangled dress and a jeweled crown and later said to her father, "Oh, Daddy, I have seen the Fairy Queen."

The king and queen toured the World's Fair and then were driven to Hyde Park. While they waited in the library for the royal arrival, Sara Roosevelt looked with disapproval at the tray of cocktails and said she was sure the king would prefer tea. When the guests arrived and came down for dinner, Eleanor reported that Franklin said, "My mother does not approve of cocktails and thinks you should have a cup of tea." The king answered as he took a cocktail, "Neither does my mother."

After church the next day they had the famous "hot dog" picnic. Eleanor had wanted to give their British guests a taste of regular American food. They also had smoked turkey which was new to Their Majesties, ham cured in different ways from different parts of the country, salads, baked beans, and strawberry shortcake.

As they left Hyde Park, standing on the rear platform of the train, the crowd sang "Auld Lang Syne." "There was something incredibly moving about this scene," Eleanor reported, "the river in the evening light, the voices of many people singing this old song, and the train slowly pulling out with the young couple waving goodbye. One thought of the clouds that hung over them and the worries they were going to face, and turned away and left the scene with a heavy heart."

For war clouds were coming ever closer. The Spanish Civil War had ended with military strongman Francisco Franco as the victor; dictator Adolf Hitler had overturned the Munich Pact and had overrun the country of Czechoslovakia ; eminent scientist Albert Einstein had written the President urging research on the atom bomb. Finally, on September 1, 1939, Franklin called Eleanor at

Hyde Park at 5 A.M. to say that Hitler had invaded Poland. And on the radio he said, "When peace has been broken anywhere, the peace of all countries is in danger."

Franklin sent peace appeals to Hitler, fascist leader Benito Mussolini and King Victor Emmanuel of Italy, and the president of Poland urging the settlement of any differences. He felt that the Pope was a strong force for peace and sent Myron Taylor as a special representative to the Vatican. But his greatest concern was that if the United States became involved we should be unprepared. He authorized an expanded air force and new naval air bases.

A year before, Eleanor had been disturbed about the world situation. After the Munich Pact, in which England and France had tried to appease rather than confront the German dictator, she had written to a friend, "It seems to me a very unsatisfactory peace and I am afraid it is not permanent."

When people told her they hoped Franklin would run for an unprecedented third term, she would smile and say she'd tell the President what they said. But privately she felt a democracy needed to be revitalized by bringing in younger leaders. Unless, as she told Joe Lash, "the international crisis made him indispensable as a stabilizing force because the people had faith in him."

When someone in the Youth Congress asked her if she would consider running for President, she answered quickly that "nothing on God's green earth could make me run." And yet she told "Hick" (Lorena Hickok) that Louis Howe "always wanted to make me President when FDR was through and insisted he could do it. You see, he was interested in his power to create personages more than in a person, tho' I think he probably cared more for me as a person as much as he cared for anyone and more than anyone else ever had."

Eleanor gave lavishly of her love to her friends, but she always retained her own independence. Her letters to Hick were full of endearments, but she also wrote, "Happiness comes through the love we give. Hick, I know you often have a feeling for me which for one reason or another I may not return in kind, but I feel I love you just the same." Eleanor's love was an unselfish devotion which grew out of her basic urge to be needed by others. She knew that some people used her to get to the President, but that made the loyalty and attentiveness of her friends even more precious.

Eleanor did not see as much of Marion and Nancy with whom she had shared the responsibility of the Todhunter School and the Val-Kill furniture factory, for the factory had been sold in 1937 and moved to East Park, and she stopped teaching at the New York school when she moved to the White House. But she remodeled the factory into a home for herself and an apartment for Miss Thompson, her secretary. Here she spent her summers when Franklin was not at the Big House, entertaining friends and learning finally to dive from the diving board.

Her children knew they could count on her if they needed her, but she often said she did not feel a closeness with any of the boys. She and Anna had become good friends. Eleanor had seen her through a divorce and marriage to John Boettinger. When Franklin, Jr., was in a hospital in Boston, she spent Christmas with him; when James had surgery at the Mayo Clinic, Eleanor was there. She worried about Elliott's divorce, about John's confusion concerning his belief in peace. He had said nothing would persuade him to fight, but now he felt he couldn't live in a world dominated by Hitler.

As the next election approached, war news from Europe was more ominous. France capitulated to the invading

German army in the spring of 1940, which led to increased defense activity in America.

Just before the drafting of civilians into the armed forces, Selective Service was begun. Negro leaders approached Eleanor with the request that Negroes be free to serve in any of the armed forces. Since Eleanor's resignation from the Daughters of the American Revolution when that organization would not allow Marian Anderson to sing in Constitution Hall, Eleanor had been hailed as champion of Negro rights. Racial prejudice had no part in her thinking, and she had often been pictured with Negro children, or at Howard University. She had invited Marian Anderson to sing at the White House and also Negro sharecroppers to talk about their problems. She considered Mary McLeod Bethune, director of the Division of Negro Affairs, a personal friend.

Now Eleanor sent the President a note suggesting he set up a conference with the leaders to get their suggestions for Negro participation in the armed forces. Later the Negro leader, Walter White, wrote to the President, "I want to send you this personal note of thanks for all you did to insure a square deal for Negroes in the Armed Forces of the United States."

Up to the time of the Democratic Convention, Franklin had not told Eleanor whether he intended to run for a third term. He did not plan to attend the convention and asked her not to go, either. She went to Val-Kill, relaxed, entertained friends, listened to the convention on the radio and to the statement Franklin had sent, saying he was not seeking the nomination. But he did not say he wouldn't accept it. Accordingly he was nominated, but the convention was snagged by Franklin's choice of Henry Wallace for Vice-President. Frances Perkins called to ask Eleanor to come to the convention. The President thought she might be a help to

Jim Farley in convincing the delegates Wallace should be his running mate.

So Eleanor flew to Chicago and found the convention in an uproar. They booed Wallace's name. Eleanor, in a blue silk dress and coat, took a seat on the platform and listened to the uproar from the delegates. They didn't want Wallace, and Franklin had said he would decline the nomination if Wallace were not chosen his running mate, for he felt Wallace was the only one who could assume the Presidency with competence if the President should not survive a third term.

When Senator Alben Barkley introduced Eleanor, the crowd applauded, but there was still a buzz of talk among the thousands gathered in the huge building. But as she spoke, the noise died. Her voice, which used to be high-pitched and shrill, had now modulated and was pleasant to listen to. She spoke in short, simple sentences, showing the delegates that they, too, had an obligation to the man they nominated for President.

"You cannot treat it as you would an ordinary nomination in an ordinary time . . . you will have to rise above considerations which are narrow and partisan. This is a time when it is the United States we fight for . . . no man who is President can carry that situation alone. This is only carried by a united people who love their country."

When Eleanor finished, the hushed crowd burst into applause. Barkley thanked her, and the balloting began. Although it was close, Wallace was the winner. Lorena Hickok and Frances Perkins, who had urged her to come to the convention, lavished their praise. "Without you we couldn't have done it," was the general consensus of the Democratic leaders.

But the praise that meant the most to Eleanor was the call that came as her plane home was taxiing to the runway. It suddenly turned back to the terminal. The President was on the phone and wanted to speak to Mrs. Roosevelt.

"You've done a good job, my dear. Thank you."

A United Press story headlined "Mrs. Roosevelt stills the tumult of 50,000." The *Daily News* reported, "Thanks to her the roll call began in a fairly dignified atmosphere . . . she has done more to soothe the convention bruises than all the astute senators."

Letters came to the White House saying her talk had "lifted the convention above petty political trading . . . and placed it on a different level." "You turned a rout into a victory." "What you said caused men of sense and honor to stop and think."

But election victory was far from won. Franklin refused to campaign, despite the issues raised by the Republican candidate, Wendell Willkie. He would stand on his record. But Eleanor had her finger on the pulse of the people and received letters imploring her to get the President to make political speeches.

She wrote him in October, "I hope you will make a few more speeches . . . the people have a right to hear your opposition to Willkie."

There was also talk that Roosevelt wanted to get the country into war. He finally issued a statement. "The purpose of our defense is defense . . . your boys are not going to be sent into any foreign wars."

Eleanor was more realistic when she wrote in her column, "No one can honestly promise you today peace at home or abroad. All any human being can do is to promise that he will do his utmost to prevent this country being involved in war."

But it was a bitter campaign, much of the abuse falling upon Eleanor, her family, the money they had made and the way they made it. There were buttons that said, "We don't

74

want Eleanor, either." Publicly she shrugged it off as political mudslinging, but she wrote to a friend, "I'll be glad when it is all over. . . . If Franklin is elected I sometimes wonder if the amount he can do will be worth the sacrifice that all of us have to make."

She was soon to find out, for with Franklin's election they were committed to four more years in the white House, years of war.

Chapter 6
War

By this time, Eleanor was used to receiving appeals for help. She routed them to the person most qualified to assist, often her husband. She helped establish the committee for the care of European children which brought them to America for the duration of the war.

With all the urgent problems of the war in Europe, she was afraid some of the successful social programs of the New Deal would be forgotten, and when she heard Congress had called the school lunch and food stamp programs "non-essential," she alerted Franklin to that fact.

Franklin appointed his wife and Mayor Fiorello LaGuardia as co-chairmen of the Office of Civilian Defense.

When Harry Hopkins returned from a six-weeks trip to England, Eleanor asked him many questions. How were the British people holding up under the steady bombing? What practical help did Churchill want from the United States? What were Britain's women doing in the war?

Eleanor was relieved when the long Congressional fight over Lend-Lease ended in victory for Franklin's plan to send military supplies to the Allies.

In August, Franklin, with a sly smile, told his wife he planned a little trip through the Cape Cod canal to do some fishing. "I knew," she said, "he was not telling me all he was going to do." She found out from Franklin, Jr., and Elliott just what the fishing trip was all about.

Elliott had been assigned to Gander Lake Field and was ordered to Argentia, Newfoundland. Franklin was an executive officer on a destroyer which accompanied merchant ships to England. He was told to report to the commander-in-chief of the U.S.S. Augusta, wondering uneasily what he had done. "When he walked on board," Eleanor related, "and saw his father it was a most pleasant surprise and a great relief." Roosevelt here met Churchill and out of this conference came the Atlantic Charter, a declaration of the common principles of the United States and Great Britain on which they based the hope for a better future for all after the war.

But in the midst of national and international crises, there were problems of illness and death. In June, Missy LeHand, Franklin's devoted young secretary, suffered a stroke, was partially paralyzed, and could not continue her work.

In September, Sara Roosevelt died. Eleanor realized that "it was a great sorrow for my husband. There was a very close bond between them in spite of the fact that he had grown away from her in some ways." Her own feelings were mixed, as in a latter to a friend she wrote, "It is dreadful to have lived so close to someone for 36 years and feel no deep affection or sense of loss. It is hard on Franklin, however."

She did say also that "my admiration for her grew through the years as I realized how many political guests she had to entertain in her house where for so many years only family and friends had been received. Mrs. Roosevelt was quite remarkable about this plunge into the national political picture and made the necessary adjustments in her life in a remarkable way."

While her mother-in-law lay dying, Eleanor was called to the bedside of her brother Hall, terminally ill with cirrhosis of the liver, a condition that results from heavy drinking. In her column after his death two weeks later she wrote, "I wish all youngsters who drink and abuse their health could see the results of great strength with the liver gone." Services were held in the White House.

Later she wrote, "As I look back on the life of this man whom I dearly loved, who never reached the heights he was capable of reaching, I cannot help having a great sense of sorrow for him, know he must often have felt deeply frustrated and disappointed by his own failure to use the wonderful gifts that were his."

After Hall's death, Eleanor plunged into work at the Office of Civilian Defense, doing her own work late at night, working on lectures, answering her mail, writing her column. It was a formidable task to organize the office and to get the various governmental agencies to cooperate. Each voluntary organization wanted to run its own show. She asked Paul Kellogg, editor of a social work magazine, for advice, and tried to follow his suggestions for making the OCD "a yeasty force for inter-agency action at the federal level, and for effective community organization throughout the country."

It has been said that all those who were alive on December 7, 1941, can remember exactly what they were doing when they heard that the Japanese had attacked the American Naval base and airfield at Pearl Harbor, in Hawaii.

Eleanor had asked about thirty people for lunch on that day and "was disappointed but not surprised when Franklin sent word a short time before lunch that he did not see how he could possibly join us." When they went upstairs after lunch, one of the ushers told them the news. The guests left, and when Eleanor went to Franklin's study, she realized he was concentrating "on what had to be done and would not talk about what had happened until this first strain was over."

After a conference with the secretaries of state, war, and navy and a naval aide, a statement was issued to the press and radio. And later, when Eleanor did get a chance to talk

Eleanor's energy was tireless before and during World War Two. Here, she is pictured with Fiorello La Guardia, Mayor of New Yorki City, whose Assistant she was in the Office of Civilian Defense.

to Franklin, "I thought in spite of his anxiety Franklin was in a way more serene than he had appeared in a long time. I think it was steadying to know finally that the die was cast. One could no longer do anything but face the fact that this country was in a war; from here on, difficult and dangerous as the future looked, it presented a clearer challenge than the long uncertainty of the past."

She said as much in her weekly radio broadcast. "We

know what we have to face and we know that we are ready to face it."

All through the evening until after midnight, members of the cabinet and congressional leaders kept coming to the President's study. The next morning Eleanor went to the Civilian Defense Office as usual, but returned to go to the Capitol with Franklin to hear him deliver a message to the joint session of Congress. He asked for a declaration of war because of this day "that will live in infamy." Eleanor thought about her "four sons of military age."

But that night she and Mayor LaGuardia boarded a plane for Los Angeles. There were rumors that the West Coast might be attacked at any moment, that Japanese submarines had surfaced off the coast of San Francisco.

They found that San Diego was the only city with a plan for civilian defense in operation. Others were waiting for the Federal government to send them money. "I hope I showed them," Eleanor said, "that getting the money was a remote possibility." But her mere presence cured people of the jitters. "It does seem to calm people down," she wrote to a friend.

Franklin thanked Eleanor for her work there, but he had agreed with his military advisors that the presence of more than 100,000 Japanese Americans on the West Coast could be dangerous. Eleanor argued, "But they are good Americans and have as much right to live there as anyone else." An editorial in a Los Angeles newspaper said she should retire from public life for championing the rights of "the treacherous snakes we call Japanese." Franklin signed the order to transfer the Nisei (American-born Japanese) to inland prison camps. They were victims of hysteria, for the FBI later found no Japanese spies in any of the Japanese American families.

A few days before Christmas Eleanor learned that British

Prime Minister Winston Churchill was expected on December 22. There was a great shifting of beds to make room for all the visitors, and Eleanor sent someone to buy gifts for the British. They arrived at the White House at 6:30, and there were seventeen for dinner.

Both Franklin and Eleanor had kept busy that day; Franklin had seen ambassadors from Russia, China, and the Netherlands and had had many other engagements; Eleanor had spent most of the day at the Office of Civilian Defense and then had attended a Salvation Army Christmas party, a Catholic Charities Christmas party, and the alley Christmas tree program, and she confessed that as the evening wore on, "I suddenly caught myself falling asleep as I sat trying to talk to my guests."

Churchill's habits were different from Franklin's. Churchill took a long nap every afternoon and then was ready to work until the early hours of the morning. Franklin had to do his regular work while Churchill slept and was often awakened when he finally did get to bed, by urgent dispatches, so Eleanor worried that "it always took him several days to catch up on sleep after Mr. Churchill left." She also reported that Churchill took two scalding hot baths a day, enjoying the soap he could not get in England. When he left he picked up $50 worth of soap to take home.

By this time the Japanese had taken Hong Kong from Britain, overrun Guam and Wake Island which were U.S. possessions, and were moving toward Manila, the capital of the Philippine Islands. In Washington statesmen from 26 nations signed an agreement that they were unified against "savage and brutal forces seeking to subjugate (rule) the world."

It seemed that people either admired or hated the Roosevelts. Franklin received mail directed to "Rattlesnake Roosevelt" and "Benedict Arnold Roosevelt" (a reference to the hero of the Battle of Saratoga in the American Revolutionary War who later turned traitor).

Eleanor worked hard at her job at the Office of Civilian Defense, but there were many who criticized her activities. When she appointed a dancer, Mayris Chaney, to develop a recreational program for children in the small space of a bomb shelter, Eleanor was attacked because the dancer's salary was $4600, and the press condemned "fan dancers" in the civilian defense program.

Because OCD headquarters stressed physical fitness, during lunch hour there was calisthenics and square dancing on the roof of the building. And the press made these "do-gooders" objects of ridicule.

They attacked Eleanor for her "communist friends and appointees," and these included the actor Melvin Douglas, head of the arts division, whom she did not appoint, and Joseph Lash, the young man from Youth Congress days who had given up his belief in communism and was working in the Youth Division of OCD.

Then there was the racial problem. Some of the southern states did not want Negroes working in the civilian defense organization. And naturally Eleanor tried to fight against the prejudice. "Unless we make the country worth fighting for by Negroes, we would have nothing to offer the world at the end of the war." She said that the war must be fought as a people's war, or "there is grave danger that it will be followed by a peace that is not a people's peace."

Eleanor learned that author Pearl Buck shared many of her ideals. The Nobel Prize-winning novelist was a trustee of Howard University, a Negro college, and she and Eleanor often spoke on civil rights issues from the same platform. Eleanor invited Miss Buck to the White House for dinner just after Madame Chiang Kai-shek, wife of the Chinese anti-communist leader, had left, and Eleanor said how interesting it had been to have Mme. Chiang for a guest. But Franklin had not shared her enthusiasm, and when he found he was to dine alone with the charming but demanding wife of the Chinese Generalissimo, he announced decisively, "Indeed I shan't; I'm going to bed early." And Eleanor added, "I don't think Franklin likes women who think they are as good as he is."

Miss Buck often wrote to the President or Eleanor about the urgency of including the Chinese in plans for a post-war world as she felt, as did Eleanor, that Anglo-Saxons planned to dominate and ignore other people. In a thank-you letter to Eleanor, Miss Buck told her how much she meant to the people "who love our country and humanity too. It is a great deal to be able to count on someone as millions of us count on you."

Because she did not hesitate to speak out on controversial issues, Eleanor's mail was heavy with letters attacking her, and one columnist said "half the trouble could be got rid of if the President would haul her (Eleanor) out of the place." But the columnist Walter Winchell reminded the people that he wished "The House of Representatives would again read the bill they voted for on December eighth. . . . It was a Declaration of War on the Axis (Hitler and Mussolini)—not Mrs. Roosevelt."

Eleanor decided to resign from the Office of Civilian Defense, and two days later she spoke as a private citizen, criticizing the "small and very vocal group of unenlightened men now under the guise of patriotism and economy, waging the age-old fight of the privileged few against the good of the many." She insisted that defense should include "better nutrition, better housing, better day-by-day medical care, better education, better recreation for every age."

Eleanor immediately turned to what she could do for the soldiers. The editor of the Junior Literary Guild's *Bulletin* asked her about her war work, and she summarized it: "I try to put as much as I can in War Bonds; to pay my debts; to do what I can for people who write about their friends and relatives in the Services and to answer the many letters from soldiers themselves. I visit hospitals and see innumerable people from other countries in order to try to find out how they are meeting their problems and pass along the information here which could be useful in meeting some of our problems."

But all of that seemed pretty ordinary, and Eleanor wanted to go to England "to see what the average household in England is going through." Franklin encouraged the idea, and arrangements were made for Eleanor and her secretary Tommy (Miss Thompson) to make the twenty-hour flight to Ireland, a short flight to Bristol and then the prime minister's special train to London.

Here they were met by the King and Queen and other officials gathered on the red carpet. They were driven to Buckingham Palace where Eleanor had a large suite and a long, narrow bedroom. At tea she met the princesses and found Elizabeth, the future queen, to be "quite serious and a child with a great deal of character and personality."

While in England Eleanor walked miles through factories, clubs and hospitals until the reporters accompanying her said they were "glassy-eyed and sagging at the knees." But Eleanor seemed tireless, appalled at the destruction caused by the bombings but learning how the British had managed civilian defense. Some of the anti-aircraft positions were handled by women. At the American Red Cross Club the soldiers and sailors called out, "Hi, Eleanor," which she accepted as a compliment, not a lack of respect, and she was soon involved hearing their complaints about the slowness of the mail, the lack of American-style food, and the absence of wool socks.

This last issue she mentioned to Supreme Allied Commander General Dwight Eisenhower the next evening, and after he had looked into the matter he wrote that they had "two and a half million pairs of light woolen socks in warehouses" and that "no man needs to march without proper footgear."

Eleanor toured naval bases, bomber squadrons, Negro troops (and was happy when their white officer said his men were the best in the Army). At some of the official lunches and dinners she met royalty-in-exile from Norway, Yugoslavia, Poland, Greece, and Czechoslovakia, and called on the Queen Mother because Franklin said she had been so nice to his mother.

She stayed with the Winston Churchills, and when she was leaving for home Mrs. Churchill came to see her with a note from the Prime Minister which said, "You certainly have left golden footprints behind you."

Eleanor was surprised and pleased to see that Franklin had taken the time to meet her plane, and in her diary that night she wrote, "I really think Franklin was glad to see me back, and I gave a detailed account of such things as I could tell quickly and answered his questions. Later I think he even read this diary and to my surprise he had also read my columns." For in the midst of all her activities in England, every day she had sent off her "My Day" column to the newspapers.

But this was to be only the beginning of her travels.

Chapter 7
The End and a New Beginning

Both Eleanor and Franklin were away from the White House several times in 1943. The President traveled to conferences in Casablanca, Quebec, Cairo, and Teheran, while Eleanor went with him to Mexico and on an inspection tour of twenty states.

Her most extensive tour was for the Red Cross to the South Pacific. Wearing a military looking Red Cross uniform, she flew in a plane christened "Our Eleanor" to seventeen islands, New Zealand, and Australia, and saw about 400,000 men in camps and hospitals.

The columnist Westbrook Pegler, always critical of Eleanor, wrote that the trip was a waste of time, a needless diversion of air power, and a cover-up of her desire to see her friend, Joe Lash.

Naval leaders had some doubts about letting the First Lady visit Guadalcanal as it was often attacked, but Eleanor pleaded to be allowed to go. "Fortunately," she wrote home later, "they bombed the night before I arrived and the night after I left." She was able to see Joe Lash, her young friend who was stationed there as a weatherman.

Reporters made much of the fact that she kissed Joe, a man who had been accused of having communist sympathies and who had actually been under surveillance during his basic training days. Eleanor knew he had renounced his youthful enthusiasm for communism several years previously, and she had continued to correspond with him and to sympathize with his personal goal of persuading Trude Pratt to marry him.

"I love you both," she had written him. "You are both fine, but you are more sensitive and less selfish than Trude. I wish I could help you gain your security and your happiness, but all I can do is send you loving thoughts many times a day. Bless you."

Joe had finally won and married Trude, and in a long letter to his wife, Lash commented, "Mrs. Roosevelt has been here and gone, a very tired Mrs. Roosevelt, agonized by the men she had seen in the hospitals, fiercely determined because of them to be relentless in working for a peace that this time will last, a very loving and motherly Mrs. Roosevelt, and despite the heat, the weariness and the tragedy, a gracious and magnificent lady."

Eleanor wrote Lash from one of her island stops, "I care first for those few people I love deeply, and then for the rest of the world, I fear. I've worked hard today, however. We were up at 3:45 and left the field at 5 and were here by 9:20. I've been to three hospitals, a big Navy recreation field, and talked to a lot of boys. I love you dearly."

She told the men, "The President feels you're doing a vital job even though some of you are not on the front lines." She sent a note to Franklin, saying that in her judgment, "Army hospitals are generally not as well equipped as those of the Navy; I also feel the officers have too much and the men too little. Malaria is as bad as the enemy and causes more casualties."

Eleanor was never satisfied that she might not have done more, but others said she took the area by storm, "saying the right thing at the right time and doing a hundred and one things that endeared her to the people."

Navy Admiral Halsey wrote later, "She alone accomplished more good than any other person or any group of civilians who had passed through this area." He said in his report that when Eleanor inspected the hospitals, "She went into every ward, stopped at every bed, and spoke to every patient. What was his name? Was there anything he needed? Could she take a message home for him? I marvelled at her hardihood, both physical and mental; she walked for miles, and she saw patients who were grievously and gruesomely wounded. But I marveled most at their expressions as she leaned over them. It was a sight I will never forget."

In the largest hospital in Australia, she told the wounded men that in the postwar world they deserved "jobs at a living wage and knowledge that the rest of the world is getting things worthwhile so your children may live in a world at peace."

She carried her own tray in the mess halls and stayed to talk with the enlisted men afterwards. Once when she came upon troops heading for the front, she spoke personally with each truckload of boys to wish them luck.

A soldier wrote to one of his Republican friends at home, "Do you think it's a cinch to come over here, and especially a woman? It's dangerous and tiresome, and it's a wonder a person her age could stand it. If those critics at home complain because her trip cost too much, we'd be willing to turn over our pay for the rest of the war to help compensate you fellows on the home front for any inconvenience you suffered by Mrs. Roosevelt's trip."

One proof of her popularity was the informality with which the servicemen greeted her. "Here comes Eleanor. Hi, Eleanor." And there were many good-natured jokes about the First Lady's popping up in out-of-the-way places.

Her days were full, and always at night she must write her column. When she finally landed in San Francisco, she took her granddaughter Sistie to lunch before flying on to New York to see Jimmy, who was leaving for duty with Admiral Nimitz.

Franklin had arranged a private lunch with Eleanor,

Eleanor during her trip in September 1943 to the Southwest Pacific to visit troops. Here she is flanked by (from left) Admiral Wiliam F. Halsey, American Red Cross Supervisor Coletta Ryan, and Admiral Willard Harmon.

which stretched out to two hours, Franklin asking what she had learned on her trip as if she were an impersonal aide reporting to her commander-in-chief. She told him she was worried about the way America was represented in the world. People were cynical and there was no more idealism. And at home, not enough was being done to relieve poverty, to treat Blacks and minorities as equals.

But Franklin, who never did like facing unpleasant

realities, was more optimistic, cautioning patience. He could always laugh, tell stories, and skirt a serious issue if he chose.

But when Eleanor went to visit the Wultwick Training School for delinquent boys and realized what had brought them to petty thievery and minor crimes, she commented to a friend, "I want primarily to get at the things that are fundamental—the social evils which create families such as those children come from." She was to make this a lifetime commitment.

Italy, one of the countries allied with Germany, had surrendered to the Allies in September, 1941, and in November there was to be a summit conference at Cairo and Teheran. Eleanor wanted to go, as she thought she might be of some help. Churchill was pushing for an Anglo-American alliance, while she felt all nations should be included. And she was afraid Franklin wouldn't hold out against Churchill's persuasive powers.

But Franklin said no, there would be no women there. He did make it possible for Elliott, Franklin, Jr., and Anna's husband John Boettinger, who were all in the European theater of war, to meet him at the conference. As it turned out, Franklin Jr., did not go, as he felt he should be with his men. His ship had been damaged, and Eleanor recorded, "I'm glad F. Jr. had the sense of responsibility and F. respected it."

Franklin's first letter upon arrival, beginning "Dearest Babs," mentioned that Madame Chiang was there with her husband, and Churchill's daughter Sarah accompanied him. He signed the letter, "Ever so much love. I wish you could be on the trip with me."

While the President was in Casablanca, the scientist Niels Bohr asked for an appointment with Eleanor. He had first visited her in July, 1943. At that time Eleanor had alerted Franklin, who suggested the eminent man talk with

Dr. Vannever Bush and Dr. James Conant of the Office of Scientific Research and Development. Now he had more than a concern about America's defense. He told her Germany had announced a secret force for destruction; an atomic bomb.

Eleanor wrote immediately to Franklin but had no reply until he reached home. Then he reassured her that America was making progress in developing the bomb. He was sure Germany could not yet use the fearsome weapon. Perhaps to divert her concern, he suggested Eleanor visit the Caribbean and South America.

While her primary purpose was to visit American troops, Eleanor also received a warm welcome from local people, especially women. One of her biographers says that women everywhere "saw her not only as a symbol of democracy and good neighborliness, but as a champion of the rights of women."

That same spring of 1944, Eleanor became alarmed at the change in Franklin's appearance. She noticed "a bluish cast to his lips and fingernails." His breathing was shallow and his hands shook when he tried to hold a coffee cup. He had a persistent cough. So, she was glad when the financier Bernard Baruch, known as the adviser to Presidents, invited Franklin to his North Carolina estate for a rest. When she and Anna visited him there, she noticed an improvement and wrote in her journal, "F. looks well but said he still has no pep. Dr. McIntire says they will do final tests when he gets home."

The doctors did not tell Eleanor that her husband had "congestive heart failure." They said he was getting better but should have more rest.

But the President knew the invasion of Europe was to take place soon, and there was little time to rest. Eleanor wrote to a friend, "I feel as though a sword were hanging over my head, dreading its fall and yet knowing it must fall to end the war. I pray that Germany will give up now that the Russians are approaching and our drive in Italy has begun. However, I have seen no encouraging signs."

Before Eleanor went to bed on June 5, 1944, Franklin told her that the invasion of mainland Europe by Allied forces was to take place at dawn. There was very little sleep for her that night, and the next day when the President publicly announced the invasion , Eleanor wrote "for hours our hearts were with the men on the beaches." But it was also a relief to know that "permanent landings have been made and that the liberation of Europe had really begun."

For a month in the summer Franklin was in Hawaii, Alaska, and the Aleutians, going over war plans with officers in the Pacific area. Eleanor spoke at various conferences about equal rights for Negroes, even in North Carolina despite "disagreeable letters and editorials" from southerners.

A Presidential election was coming up in the fall. Eleanor did not oppose Franklin's decision to run again, realizing he felt he had to finish the job and win the war. "He'll go on as long as the people want him," she said.

She was as concerned as Franklin over what would happen after the war. She was chairman of a conference on "How Women May Share in Postwar Policy Planning." And she invited Walter Reuther, labor leader, to give her his ideas on the way industries could convert to peace-time products.

Eleanor was in favor of Henry Wallace's being nominated again for Vice-President, but the Democratic Party picked Harry Truman, the Senator from Missouri. Truman kept insisting he didn't want the job, but he had the backing of various labor leaders, and he was nominated.

When the Republicans selected Thomas E. Dewey, she worried that if he should win, all of Franklin's reforms would be lost. She wrote to James, "I am only concerned because Dewey seems to me more and more to show no understanding of the job at home or abroad."

She urged Franklin to campaign more vigorously. And by election night Franklin could tell his Hyde Park neighbors who always came by torchlight procession to be with the President, "It looks like I'll be coming up here from Washington again for another four years."

"There was a great deal of excitement all through the evening," Eleanor wrote afterwards, "but I can't say that I felt half as excited as I will feel the day that I hear the war is over." Dewey did not admit defeat until 3:15 in the morning.

Franklin left for the Yalta Conference, a sort of summit meeting with Churchill and Russian ally Joseph Stalin, two days after the inauguration, and before he left the Crimea he wrote his wife, "Dearest Babs," that he thought the conference had been successful, though "I am a bit exhausted but really all right."

But he was not all right. His face was gray, his hands shook, and he was anxious to get to Warm Springs where he could rest and relax. After he left, Eleanor wrote to a friend, "I say a prayer daily that he may be able to carry on till we have peace and our feet are set in the right direction."

Meanwhile, people kept calling on Eleanor for help: poor farmers who were about to lose their homes, soldiers, veterans, Negroes, Jewish refugees, nuclear scientists—all spoke to her about their needs and she always responded with practical action.

On April 12, she held her usual press conference and answered questions about the San Francisco Conference soon to take place to organize the United Nations. Her luncheon guest was a lecturer for Russian war relief. A little after 3 P.M., while she was talking to an adviser to the U.S. delegation to the San Francisco Conference, the phone rang.

Laura Delano (Polly), the President's cousin, was calling from Warm Springs. The President had fainted. Eleanor asked a few questions, ended the interview with her caller, and spoke to Dr. McIntire, Franklin's physician in Washington. He thought there was no cause for alarm, but suggested they fly to Warm Springs later in the day. She should keep her other appointments in order not to alarm the public.

It was after she had spoken at a benefit for the Thrift Shop that she was called to the phone. Steve Early, the press secretary, urged her to come home immediately. She said afterwards, "I knew in my heart something dreadful had happened . . . and sat with clenched hands all the way to the White House."

Steve Early told her that the President had "slipped away" that afternoon. "Somehow," she recorded later, "in emergencies one moves automatically." There were things to be done. She sent a wire to the boys: "Father slipped away. He would expect you to carry on and finish your jobs. Love, Mother."

She sent for the Vice-President, and when he arrived, noted, "I could think of nothing to say except how sorry I was for him, how much we would all want to help him in any way we could, and how sorry I was for the people of the country, to have lost their leader and friend before the war was really won."

Eleanor flew to Warm Springs with Steve Early and Dr. McIntire. It was after midnight when they walked into the "Little White House" cottage. She embraced Polly, Margaret Stuckley, who had been devoted to Franklin, and Grace Tully. It was obvious they were all in a state of shock. There didn't seem to be much they could tell her.

The President had been sitting for his portrait, joking and planning to attend a barbecue in the afternoon, when he suddenly said, "I have a terrific headache," put a hand up to his neck, and slumped forward. He never regained consciousness.

Eleanor went into the bedroom and closed the door behind her. The face of the man on the bed was distorted by the cerebral hemorrhage. The coffin must be kept closed. The public would remember Franklin only as he had been, the warm smile, the jaunty tilt of his head.

Something was missing from the account of Franklin's last day. Why was his portrait being painted? For whom? Who was in the room with him? Why did they delay in calling the White House? Polly had known when she called at nearly 3:30 P.M. that Franklin was dying. Were they hiding something?

Eleanor had trained herself to be a good observer when she went on inspection trips for Franklin, and her questions could be penetrating until she knew the truth. She questioned the doctors, the cook and the rest of the staff, Polly, Grace, and Margaret. From the conflicting stories of how many were with him when he collapsed and exactly what time it was, she pieced together there were two more people with Franklin who had left soon after the stroke, the portrait painter and someone else no one wanted to mention.

Finally Polly told her. Lucy Mercer Rutherford. But she hastened to add that although Franklin had seen a great deal of Lucy when Eleanor was out of town, she was sure the relationship never went beyond enjoyment of each other's company. She saw nothing wrong in that.

In Elliott's account of that time, he said, "Mother would not allow herself to show any signs of distress." And she never mentioned Lucy in her own version of those tragic days. She said only, "I decided to accept the fact that a man must be what he is, life must be lived as it is . . . you cannot live at all if you do not learn to adapt yourself to your life as it happens to be.

"All human beings have failings, all human beings have needs and temptations and stresses. Men and women who live together through long years get to know one another's failings; but they also come to know what is worthy of respect and admiration in those they live with and in themselves."

On the train back to Washington, Eleanor lay in her berth with the window shade up, watching the silent and often weeping crowds in the stations who had come to honor the President's funeral car. For them, she reasoned later, "This was a sorrow of all those to whom he had been a symbol of strength and fortitude." In the East Room of the White House, the bronze coffin was opened for Eleanor to say a final goodbye and place a few flowers beside the body of the man to whom she had been married for forty years. She wore the golden fleur-de-lis pin Franklin had given her as a wedding present.

Franklin had wanted to be buried in the Rose Garden at Hyde Park, so there was another service there. Eleanor stayed long enough to greet her personal friends and the officials, and went back on the train with the new President and Mrs. Truman to begin the process of moving from the White House.

The first few weeks after her husband's death, Eleanor kept busy, moving out of the White House in a few days, unloading the boxes at Hyde Park and watching the spring come. On the second floor sleeping porch at Val-Kill, she woke to the morning sounds of birds and looked through the new green and blush of the maples to the sun glinting on the lake. She took Fala (Franklin's little dog, named after an old Scotch ancestor of the President) on walks through the woods, and he accepted her companionship as he had that of his master.

The First Couple had decided to give the Big House to the government, and that meant clearing it of anything the family personally wanted. She took her own money and bought Val-Kill and over 800 acres of farmland from the estate, as the executors had to sell to the highest bidder. "I could not bear not to try to hold the land in case some child might want to run it some day," she said.

Franklin had already set up the first Presidential Library on sixteen acres of the property donated by his mother. Here he had placed his letters (he sometimes received 4000 a day), pictures, ship models and books, fifty million items in all. Here scholars would come to do their research on the Roosevelt years.

But when the settling of the estate was done, what was she to do? She wanted to keep on with her page for the *Ladies' Home Journal* and her daily column for the newspapers. She was urged to run for the U.S. Senate, but refused immediately. She and President Truman sent letters to each other frequently, sometimes about personalities, sometimes on issues. He seemed to value her opinion and advice.

She joined a newly formed Citizens Committee, but what she really wanted to do was to help carry out Franklin's ideas for a lasting peace. After the dropping of the atomic bombs on Hiroshima and Nagasaki, she was more than ever convinced of the need for international control and safeguards against such awesome power being misused.

The first meeting of the United Nations Assembly was to be held in London, and President Truman asked her to become a delegate. Eleanor protested that she'd had no real experience in foreign affairs, and "I didn't know much about parliamentary procedure."

But Truman reassured her that her presence there would remind other delegates of Franklin's high hopes for the organization. When he put it that way, she could only agree that perhaps it was her duty to accept.

A columnist wrote about her appointment, that other women could represent America, "but this is a good appointment because she, better than perhaps any other person, can represent the little people of this country, indeed of the world."

But her old enemy, the columnist Westbrook Pegler, thought the country wasn't getting its money's worth; the delegates got more salary than a senator.

In response to the appointment, she said she would take with her "a sincere desire to understand the problems of the rest of the world and our relationship to them; a real good will for people throughout the world; a hope that I shall be able to build a sense of personal trust and friendship with my co-workers."

It was by no means an easy job.

Chapter 8

The United Nations Call

A tall figure dressed in mourning black got out of a taxi and hurried up the gangplank of the *Queen Elizabeth* to join the other delegates leaving for the London conference. The newsreel cameras and microphones that had recorded the entrances and speeches of the other distinguished delegates had left, and with no fanfare or ceremony, Eleanor Roosevelt boarded the ship as a private citizen.

During the voyage she took long walks around the decks with her fellow delegates, discussing the issues to be ironed out at the conference. She read all the pages of materials the State Department had provided. A reporter for the *New York Times* wrote that Mrs. Roosevelt had impressed her colleagues "by her industry in studying technical details."

Eleanor's hotel room in London was filled with flowers and letters of welcome from the King and Queen, the Churchills, other officials she had entertained in the White House, and friends from her school days at Allenswood. she made time for some social visits, although she told the Royal Family she couldn't stay long because she had to get back to work.

She had been assigned to Committee III dealing with cultural, social, and humanitarian issues. Most of the members of the U.S. delegation were Senators or former Senators, and they weren't too happy to have "an emotional, rattle-brained woman" as their associate, but they did a complete about-face by the end of the conference.

Eleanor had her own thoughts about the men. She wrote to a friend that both Arthur Vandenberg and John Foster

Dulles "have no confidence, so they are rude and arrogant and create suspicion . . . Jimmy Byrne's overconfidence isn't right either. Why can't we be natural?"

She tried to be cordial toward the Russians, but she and Vishinsky, the chief Soviet delegate, held opposite opinions on many issues, especially the refugee problem. There were about a million people, displaced persons from the war years, facing death if they were returned to the country from which they had escaped. To the Russians, they were traitors. Eleanor felt they should have freedom of choice and not be forced to be repatriated against their will.

The debates went on for days. Vandenberg and Dulles admitted to friends that they were amazed at Mrs. Roosevelt's "patience and good judgment." On the final vote, taken at 1 A.M., the United States had won, a triumph, Eleanor felt, for her belief in human dignity.

Largely because of that victory, the Economic and Social Council of the U.N. asked her to serve on the Human Rights Commission, and she was quickly acclaimed chairman.

Eleanor was also useful in other areas. Once when the French delegate spoke for twenty minutes and the translator couldn't follow, Eleanor, still fluent in French, offered to give the "essential meaning" of his speech and translated competently.

President Truman asked her to continue with the delegation when the U.N. met again in October. The summer before, Eleanor tried to work on the second book of her autobiography. She told her friends it bored her to write about herself, but she thought she had an obligation to history to write about Franklin's years in the White House.

In August Eleanor had an automobile accident. She wrote in her column the next day that she had grown sleepy, collided with another car, and sideswiped a third. No one was seriously injured, though Eleanor's front teeth were broken. "I am black and blue pretty much all over . . . but now I shall have two lovely porcelain teeth which will look far better than the rather protruding large ones which most of the Roosevelts have." Her family agreed that the new teeth were a great improvement.

In January 1947, President Truman appointed Eleanor to a four-year term with the Human Rights Commission, and again she was elected chairman. Of course her ideas and those of the communists were quite different. The Yugoslav representative said the ideals of the middle class were obsolete. He believed individuals could only be considered as members of a group.

Eleanor wanted a Declaration of Rights that would include those in the American Declaration of Independence and Bill of Rights. But the American delegation had to accept the fact that Eastern nations such as Russia and China might have a different view of "rights." They must draft a statement which all fifty-five nations could accept.

The following December when the Commission met in Geneva, Switzerland, the American delegation was faced with a Russian demand to investigate charges of discrimination against Negroes in the United States.

A *Times* reporter said the Russians gave the U.S. a very hard time, but "they seem to have met their match in Mrs. Roosevelt. Their attacks [become] flurries in the face of her calm and undisturbed but often pointed replies."

Eleanor's tactics were to admit there were some good points in the Russian argument, but to say, "America is willing to have U.S. practices investigated if Russia would allow us to do the same in the Soviet Union." Nothing more was heard on that subject.

Every word was discussed thoroughly. The first article read, "All men are created equal," until the delegate from India, Mrs. Hansen Mehta, objected. She felt that excluded

Eleamor Roosevelt during her tenure as Chairman of the United Nations Human Rights Commission.

women, that the phrase would be taken literally by the men in her country. The commission voted unanimously that the phrase should read "all people" instead of "all men."

The word "created" was also a problem, and it was changed to "are born," because the Communists did not believe in a Supreme Being who could "create" man.

The week before Christmas the Declaration of Human Rights was approved by a vote of 13–4. As the delegates said goodbye, the Russian, Bogomolov, confessed he was very tired, but he told Eleanor, "You look fresh as a daisy."

There was still more work to be done at the 1948 session of the Commission. Russians wanted to investigate poor housing and high medical costs in the United States. Eleanor agreed cordially if they would permit the U.S. to look into those conditions in Russia. Again, the Russians backed down.

The draft of the Declaration was finally accepted on June 18, with the Soviet bloc not voting. The U.N. Department of Public Information paid tribute to Mrs. Roosevelt, who had "guided and inspired the work of the U.N. in the field of human rights."

The 1948 General Assembly met in September in Paris, and Eleanor was asked to speak on "The Struggle for the Rights of Man." The basic obstacle to peace, she said, was the different ideas of human rights held by the Soviet Union. "The issue of human liberty is as decisive now as it was . . . at the time of the American Revolution."

It was not until December 10 that the Assembly adopted the Resolution, with Soviet bloc nations not voting. The assembly delegates gave Eleanor a standing ovation.

Eleanor's name was proposed for the Nobel Prize, the first of several nominations, but it was never awarded to her despite President Kennedy's statement in 1961 that she was "a living symbol of world understanding and peace."

Eleanor had found the Russians difficult to deal with, but she said she operated in four principles: "Have convictions; be friendly; stick to your beliefs as they stick to theirs; work as hard as they do."

Eleanor had not approved of Churchill's speech in

Missouri in 1946 calling for an Anglo-American military alliance to combat the "iron curtain." She felt it was more important to build a strong U.N. organization than for the three great powers, England, Russia, and the United States, to build up their individual military strength. Although all three nations said they wanted peace, they did not trust each other. Eleanor feared the nation was paying more attention to the wishes of the Army and Navy than to the State Department, and that Truman was leaning too far toward Churchill's ideas and away from Franklin's plans for post-war Europe.

Elliott wrote a book, "As He Saw It," about his father's efforts for peace. He now saw these efforts being undermined by British imperialism and American militarism against Russia. Eleanor defended Elliott's right to his opinion, but her experience with Russians led her to feel he was being used by the Communists.

Eleanor's own stand was apparent when she joined with other liberals to form an American non-Communist group that would be both liberal and progressive. Americans for Democratic Action was born. "If we fail to meet our problems here, no one else in the world will do so," she said. "If we fail, the heart goes out of progressives throughout the world."

The U.S. policy known as the Truman Doctrine disturbed Eleanor. It supported free people who were trying to resist being taken over by outside forces and proposed sending aid to Greece and Turkey. She agreed with Truman that communism follows economic chaos, but she felt that the best hope for peace lay with the United Nations, and that that was the organization that should have handled the problem rather than the United States alone. Senator Vandenberg agreed with her. "The Administration made a colossal blunder in ignoring the U.N.," he wrote.

The Marshall Plan, massive economic aid to help Europe after the devastation of World War II, was a better solution; as she pointed out, it "is a bona fide offer to help Europe to get back on its feet." Eleanor admired General George Marshall's "integrity and his deep convictions," she wrote in "My Day," saying, "He is a good democrat in the best sense of the word, and he wants to get on with the business of creating a peaceful world in which you and I and all the people can have a chance for a better life."

As head of the United Nations General Assembly, Marshall consulted with Eleanor at many points. She was worried that a war with Russia might break out any minute. In February, 1948, there was no more democracy in Czechoslovakia when armed communists took over the government.

Eleanor wrote Marshall, sending a copy to President Truman, urging a conference with Russia "before we have a third World War." In U.N. meetings she reported that the Russians "seem to want to see nothing accomplished," and she wrote to a friend, "I think it will take a long time to get real understanding with the USSR government. It will be the result of long and patient work. Their government and its representatives think differently. They will have to reach a higher standard of living and not be afraid to let others in and their own out before we can hope for a change."

Eleanor had tried being patient and understanding with the Soviets, but she realized they looked on her attitude as weakness, and she determined never to compromise again. For this strength, Vishinsky called her a meddling old woman. But a shooting war did not develop.

Eleanor was in Paris for a session of the U.N. during the Presidential elections of 1948. The newspapers all expected Republican Thomas E. Dewey to win, and Europeans were amazed when Truman was re-elected. The correspondents asked Eleanor if the U.S. press was controlled and deliberately misled the people. That gave Eleanor an opportunity to point out that both the press and the people were completely independent. They wrote what they believed and voted as they pleased.

The last session of the U.N. in Paris that Eleanor attended was in the fall of 1951 that continued into 1952. Toward the end of the session, the chairman, Ambassador Austin, became ill and Eleanor presided over the American delegation. She continued to serve until a new Republican administration was elected in 1952. All delegates resigned so that the new President, Dwight D. Eisenhower, could be free to appoint his own choice of delegates. Those who were Democrats were not re-appointed. Eleanor volunteered to work with the American Association for the United Nations to keep in touch with the one organization she felt could work for peace.

Instead of returning home across the Atlantic, Eleanor decided to take the long way around the world and visit India by way of Lebanon, Syria, Jordan, and Israel.

Eleanor had not been in favor of the 1948 partitioning of Palestine into separate Jewish and Arab states. The problem of Jews in refugee camps should be debated and solved within the U.N., she felt. But when she saw the United States moving toward establishing a temporary trusteeship, she felt strongly that that position would undermine the authority of the U.N. even more. She offered her resignation as a delegate to President Truman because she felt she must criticize the policies of the Administration.

Truman begged Eleanor not to resign, for the U.N. and the country needed her. He had heard that Russia was about to recognize the Jewish State, and without consulting even his ambassador to the United Nations, Truman announced

America's recognition of that State. And in May, 1949, Israel was voted a member of the United Nations.

Eleanor had never been in any of the Near Eastern countries, and when she left Paris for the long trip back to New York, she flew directly to Beirut, Lebanon, the most Westernized of the Arab countries. "It was a beautiful and peaceful-looking city," she wrote in her autobiography. Lebanon's hills were "so carefully cultivated in tiny plots, and there were many signs of important archaeological exploration in this ancient part of the civilized world."

Eleanor flew to Damascus, Syria, and visited the home of a workman, sparsely furnished except for a few couches around the bare room. From him she learned about conditions in his country. Newsmen she talked to were violently opposed to Israel and couldn't see her point that after World War I, the Balfour Declaration favored the establishment of a Jewish state, and both the United States and Great Britain had agreed to it. But the Arabs talked about "wiping out Israel."

In Amman, Jordan, Eleanor visited Palestinian refugee camps. Comparing them with German refugee camps full of displaced Jews, she found the Arab camps "distressing beyond words." The people seemed to have no hope and nothing to do. In contrast, Jewish people in camps all had the hope of going to Israel and starting life anew.

And going from the Arab countries to Israel "was like breathing the air of the United States again. . . . I felt I was among people . . . dedicated to fulfilling a purpose." She was impressed with the progress in health services, in reclaiming the desert and making it productive, and in developing the country industrially.

Eleanor described her trip to Pakistan and India in a book "India and the Awakening East." She had first had the invitation to India when Prime Minister Nehru had visited

Hyde Park. The invitation was renewed, and a huge crowd had gathered at the airport in Karachi. During her stay people knelt in the street as she passed. Her modest comment later was, "I hadn't realized how they cared about Franklin."

In her thirty-day tour, Eleanor visited important cities, lectured veiled Moslem women about America's League of Women Voters, and how influential women could be. She addressed Parliament in New Delhi, comparing India's problems with those of America in its beginnings and expressing sympathy for India's need for neutrality.

When Eleanor returned to the U.S., she gave President Truman a report of her visits, urging him to approve economic aid to India and Pakistan if they were to develop strong and stable governments. Such a policy would pay greater dividends than money spent on military aid, she felt. Ambassador to India Chester Bowles wrote that she had done much to increase understanding of the United States foreign objectives, and that she had made a deep impression, particularly among students and the press. Her visit was "a tremendous success."

But there was more to come.

Chapter 9
Expansion of "My Day"

It had been hard for the women of Japan to adjust to the new democracy, overseen by Duglas MacArthur, the U.S.had imposed on them after the war. They had been taught from childhood that the role of women was to serve men. They must revere the Emperor as a god. Now everything had changed. Women needed to be educated in what part they could play to make democracy work. What better teacher of democracy could they find than Eleanor Roosevelt?

In the spring of 1953 Eleanor was invited to Japan to talk to groups of Japanese men and women about democracy in America. With her went Miss Corr, her secretary since the faithful Tommy had recently died, and Elliott's wife Minnewa. Minnewa "proved to be a good traveling companion and we enjoyed many delightful experiences together," Eleanor recorded.

The group spent five weeks in Japan, which gave Eleanor an appreciation of the complex problems facing a defeated nation trying to maintain its pride. The students she spoke to asked many questions, and each session took a long time because everything had to be translated.

To the question, "Why did your country use the atom bomb?" Eleanor explained that the leaders felt it would end the war quickly, but she always added her own feeling of horror at any kind of warfare. Nations must never go to war again; they must all work for peace, because, she wrote to a friend, "if there is another Pearl Harbor, there will be undoubtedly another Hiroshima."

From the man who had been the Japanese ambassador to

Washington at the time of Pearl Harbor , Eleanore received a hand-written note saying he had never lied to President Roosevelt, that he had not known about the Pearl Harbor attack in advance. Eleanor answered his letter: "I know my husband always felt you had been honest with him. I remember his saying so. . . I hope we will have an opportunity to discuss how best we can improve relationships between our two countries."

There were questions on how to interpret the "right to work" phrase in the Constitution. The United States thought the government must be responsible for an economic climate so that anyone who wanted work could find it. And if people wouldn't work through no fault of their own, the government should create jobs rather than let people starve. This is what Franklin had done in the New Deal years to relieve the Depression problems.

But the Russians felt that since the government controlled all jobs, the government was responsible for seeing that people not only had jobs but worked at them. Here there was no freedom as the West understood it, no equality under the law. How were the Japanese to interpret this article of the Human Rights Declaration of the United Nations?

Since Eleanor was largely responsible for that Declaration, she did her best to explain what it meant to her and to democratic nations.

But there were long-standing customs which had never been a bit democratic. For instance, the mother-in-law in a Japanese family ruled the lives of each member (except her husband and eldest son) in anything but a democratic manner. She controlled the order in which the family took their baths, with the daughter-in-law always last. She also controlled the money, each wage-earner giving her his wages. She decided who should spend the money and how it should be spent.

In the final report of her visit Eleanor wrote, "It is difficult to see, with the family system still untouched in rural areas and in the poorer areas, how great changes are going to happen quickly." But she felt a lack of leadership from upper-class groups. The students needed counseling, and so did the women. "Everywhere the women were willing to talk," she wrote. "I think my being here has given the women quite a lift and added to their sense of confidence and importance."

Eleanor met with Prime Minister Yoshida, whom she decided "was not progressive in our sense of the word." She talked with Princess Chichibu, the Emperor's widowed sister-in-law, who was genuinely concerned about the condition of women workers in factories and on farms.

Elenor had requested an interview with the Emperor and Empress, and this was granted on the day she was to leave Japan. She must wear a dress with long sleeves, or at least with gloves that reached to three-quarter-length sleeves. She must follow their Majesties' lead in standing, sitting, and bowing and speak only when spoken to.

"I am afraid," Eleanor confessed in writing about the experience, "that I did not observe the rule that one should speak only when spoken to. I asked a few questions myself, or rather I made some remarks intended to draw out the ideas of the Empress."

Eleanor mentioned that the women of Pakistan and India were drawing closer together as they learned more about each other, and perhaps that could be true of the women in other countries. The Empress agreed that more education was needed for changes, but she was afraid, when these changes came, that real values might be lost.

Eleanor agreed there was that danger, but she thought it

less dangerous when intelligent, broad-minded, and educated women took the lead in bringing about the necessary changes.

Eleanor realized the difficulties inherent in establishing a democratic form of government in Japan and "especially of educating women to take an active part in public affairs."

Leaving Japan, Eleanor and Maureen flew to Hong Kong, Istanbul, and Greece, while Minnewa went to Hawaii to meet Elliott.

The State Department made arrangements for their goodwill ambassador to be entertained by heads of state. In Hong Kong, Governor Grantham invited Eleanor to dinner and included several Chinese dignitaries who had escaped to Hong Kong. One of the chief topics of conversation was the plight of refugees.

The Governor offered to have her driven to the border of Communist China. The road wound through vegetable gardens, rice paddies, and small villages of the "New Territories" until they reached a bridge guarded only by a handful of soldiers and a few strands of barbed wire. Despite the barrier, many Chinese escaped to Hong Kong every day. Some, she was told, walked miles along the railroad until they found an unguarded place to cross the border.

Hong Kong tried to make room for these refugees. At first they lived in hillside holes, collecting tin, tar paper, scrap lumber, and sacking to make flimsy shelters. Whole families lived with no sewage and no water supply. All water had to be carried a long way. The contrast between the Governor's white mansion in a gardened park and the huts on the hillside was acute. But overcrowded Hong Kong was trying, gradually, to provide many-story concrete resettlement developments to house the people. Many also lived on tightly packed boats in harbors on Hong Kong Island.

Even the space between mainland Kowloon and Hong

112

Kong Island was crowded, not only with Star Ferry boats shunting back and forth, but with cargo ships, tall master junks, little sampans poled by one person, usually an old woman, ships of the Navy, a large cruise ship.

Eleanor talked to two men from Taipei where Chiang Kai-shek had set up his government and planned to retake China some day. They asked her if she planned to visit Taipei. But since she had entertained Mme. Chiang in the White House, it would be impossible to be in Taiwan and not see the Generalissimo's wife. "But I knew that if I saw her," she recorded later, "I would have to tell her I did not think her dream of regaining China was possible. I felt that Chiang Kai-shek had had his chance and had not used the right methods to unify the country. And I did not believe he any longer had a chance to do so."

After short hiatuses in New Delhi, Turkey and Greece, the last stop on their tour was a short hop to Yugoslavia where Eleanor had an appointment to interview dictator Marshall Josef Broz Tito at his summer home on the wooded island of Brioni.

Yugoslavia had fought Germany and embraced communism, but of a different variety from that of Russia. When Eleanor talked to factory workers, she learned that half of the profits were divided among the workers, an incentive to increased production. Industries were operated by councils of workers, a kind of compromise between communist and capitalist ideas.

A farm woman who had two cows and a little vegetable garden told Eleanor that she and her six grandchildren ate mostly butter, cheese, and bread she had made, but little meat. Although the government gave farmers tools and fertilizer, most of them were slow to accept new ways.

Eleanor visited hospitals with modern research facilities, most of which had been supplied by the U.N. or the United

States, she was told. Everywhere she found that people asked penetrating questions of her, showing they were aware of what was going on in the world.

Eleanor described her journey to Brioni as "one of the most delightful days I spent" (in Yugoslavia). She, Maureen, and Doctor/friend David Gurewitsch went by plane to the seacoast, by automobile to a point opposite the island, by boat across the water, and by an old-fashioned carriage to the villa.

The man who came to greet her "seemed far too youthful" to be the head of government, but she observed later that his hair was graying and there were "deep lines of experience in his strongly molded face."

Eleanor asked if he thought the people were contented under his Socialist form of government. He was honest enough to say that probably not everyone was content, for the government had nationalized the property of landowners, but he felt, on the whole, that people realized the government was doing things that would be best for the country in the long run.

Eleanor was curious how communism worked in Yugoslavia. "Communism really exists nowhere," Tito told her, "least of all in the Soviet Union." Communism was an idea, he maintained, that could only be achieved when people cease to be selfish and greedy and when everyone receives according to his needs from communal production. That ideal was a long way off.

Tito did not consider himself a dictator. Laws were published in the papers before being sent to Parliament, and thus they could be discussed and altered. His aim was to rebuild his country, and he realized, he said, that to improve the standard of living, peace was essential.

The Marshall took them all to another island for lunch, piloting the speedboat himself. In the afternoon he invited them for a short trip on the state yacht in the Adriatic Sea, pointing out various landmarks along the coast. But he did not move in public without security, as there were armed ships nearby and military airplanes overhead.

Eleanor concluded that Yugoslavia did not want world domination and that Tito was a powerful leader with long-range plans for self-government by the people. But she decided that much of the future would depend on the United States and how well "we could prove that our democracy is concerned about and benefits the people."

Could the next election affect changes for the better?

Chapter 10

First Lady of the World

Eleanor never liked to have people make a fuss over her birthdays, but she made an exception for her seventieth. The American Association for the U.N. wanted to give her a party at the Hotel Roosevelt to raise money for the organization. This fund-raising event might well get them out of debt.

Sharing the platform were Dag Hammerskjold, United Nations Secretary General; Trygve Lie, who had held that position formerly; New York Senator Herbert Lehman; her old friend Bernard Baruch; Mayor Robert Wagner; Dr. Ralph Bunche, Director of the Trusteeship Department of the U.N.; and her neighbor and former Secretary of the Treasury, Henry Morgenthau, Jr. Andrei Vishinsky, permanent delegate for the Soviet Union at the U.N., also attended, reminding Eleanor of the many times their wills had clashed over the wording of the Declaration of Human Rights in 1948. His presence she interpreted "as an apology for his rude behavior at that time."

Edward R. Murrow, commentator for the Columbia Broadcasting System, was master of ceremonies and read messages of congratulations from many world leaders.

The *New York Times* the next day showed a picture of Eleanor cutting the multi-tiered birthday cake decorated at the base with the flags of all nations. The *Times* reported Senator Lehman's speech in which he praised all of the humanitarian crusades Eleanor had undertaken. "You have become a symbol of those qualities of mind and heart which are called compassion and humanitarianism. Those qualities find expression in the concept of brotherhood and of universality—of the fundamental equality of all men and women in the eyes of God."

Eleanor's response was a plea for more recognition of that equality. "We need never stop until we feel that everyone at home has justice, equality of opportunity, and that respect which is due all human beings. I would like to see us meet the world's peoples openly."

Eleanor went on to say that more than achievement she treasured the love and respect of her children and grandchildren.

When a reporter for the *Herald Tribune* asked if she planned to slow down now that she was seventy, she said, "No, I haven't slackened my pace. At least, not yet . . . At seventy, the advantage is you take life more calmly. You know that this, too, shall pass.'"

Eleanor's activities in the 1956 Presidential campaign for Democratic candidate Adlai Stevenson actually increased. After his defeat in 1952, Stevenson had taken a trip around the world to study conditions in other countries. On her own world trips Eleanor found that leaders praised Stevenson's statesmanship and his ability to listen in order to learn the facts. She told him that in the field of international relations "I cannot think of anyone else who has the ability to do the job you could do in meeting the most vital needs of today."

On the domestic field Eleanor suggested he learn more about what the common people were thinking and feeling. "Get a small automobile and travel in various sections of the country," she said, "and stay in each area until you can feel what they are feeling."

But Stevenson did not have Franklin's easy way with political crowds. Furthermore, former President Truman had endorsed Averill Harriman, who had held many political positions including governor of New York State. Eleanor had always liked Truman, and when they met for lunch they agreed that each must do what he thought was right.

Eleanor did what she could to assure her candidate's nomination, attending a reception Stevenson gave in her honor, a luncheon for women delegates, and a meeting of the platform committee to speak on civil rights and education. She also spoke at the convention itself. Although she thought she had done poorly because there was so much noise she could scarcely be heard, Edward R. Murrow called it "the greatest convention speech I ever heard." She urged Democrats to "go beyond the New Deal and the Fair Deal and start a campaign to truly end poverty in America."

Eleanor then took off for three weeks in Europe, intending to come back, keep her lecture appointments, and perhaps take a minor part in the election campaign. It didn't work out that way. "The two months after my return proved to be the most hectic in my life," she admitted.

In one day in Portland, Eleanor had an interview on television, went to a political cocktail party, a dinner in her honor, an evening radio talk, a reception at the Masonic Temple, and at 11 P.M. a recording to be broadcast later with four high school students.

The next day she flew to San Francisco, wrote two newspaper columns, spoke in Oakland, was guest of honor at a dinner, got back to San Francisco late that night, and caught a plane for Los Angeles at seven o'clock the next morning. Here she spoke at a luncheon, held a news conference, attended a reception, wrote two newspaper columns, introduced via television Governor Stevenson speaking in Milwaukee, and flew to San Diego for a televised debate with Senator Thomas Kuchel of California.

But the day wasn't yet over. Eleanore held a press conference, went to a reception where she had to shake hands with about two thousand people, flew back to Los Angeles at 10:30 P.M., and an hour later boarded a plane for New York, "with my shoes off," she reported happily.

In the interlude before resuming campaigning in West Virginia, she spoke to the West Point cadets on "World Affairs," did some recordings to be used in Mayor Wagner's campaign for mayor of New York City, and entertained a dozen people for dinner.

In West Virginia Eleanor stopped to talk to the miners, something she had not done since the 1930s. She went to Michigan, Wisconsin, Illinois, Minnesota, New York, and finally to Washington, D.C., where she was on a television program with Senator Margaret Chase Smith at 5:30 and in St. Louis that evening. She got back to Hyde Park just in time to cast her vote for Stevenson.

The outcome was disappointing, though she had never fooled herself about the difficulties of defeating Eisenhower's bid for a second term. Still, she said, "I felt sad because I am a strong admirer of Governor Stevenson and I believed his abilities were needed to meet the problems that would arise in the next four years. But I knew that somehow those problems would be met and I was pleased that I could at least say to myself that I had done all I had been asked to do, and all I could do."

In 1957 the Sultan of Morocco invited Eleanor for a visit. With Dr. Gurewitsch and his daughter, Elliott and his wife, and several friends, she flew to Casablanca, staying at the same hotel where the famous conference of Franklin and Churchill had been held during the war. Since Elliott had been with his father at that conference, he knew the area.

At the capital, Rabat, the young Sultan, welcomed them, told them how much he had admired FDR and offered to let them make a tour of the country. He seemed interested in working out solutions to the Arab-Jewish hostilities.

From Marrakech, Elliott reported they bounced along dirt tracks "that took us past camel herds hundreds strong and ox-powered water wheels irrigating patches of green in the drab desert." They saw sheep driven by by hooded peasants "through the swirling dust." And outside one town a crowd waited in the hot sun shouting their welcome and holding up a sign that said, "We always remember President Roosevelt."

Eleanor wrote afterward, "The more I traveled throughout the world, the more I realized how important it is for Americans to see with understanding eyes the other peoples of the world whom modern means of communication and transportation are constantly making closer neighbors." But she felt, too, the responsibility that America has, for "the world is looking to us for leadership."

But on a visit to the Soviet Union in 1957, she confessed to being almost frightened by "many things that showed how hard we must strive if we are to maintain our position of world leadership."

Eleanor was most anxious to interview the new leader of the USSR, Nikita Khrushchev. She was plagued by a few ailments like arthritis and a hearing loss and wanted Dr. Gurewitsch and his wife to go on the trip with her. He also spoke Russian, took excellent pictures, and managed a tape recorder, making him a valuable traveling companion.

They saw Lenin's tomb, a ballet, a circus, a state farm, hospitals, the walled city of Samarkland, a Leningrad medical school and the Pavlov Institute, a home for orphaned children. Here even the babies were being taught to do simple exercises and older children did more complicated routines all by themselves without instruction. Eleanor realized that children were being trained to accept discipline at an early age.

From this she drew a parallel with world affairs.

"Because of life-long conditioning," she wrote, "the government can depend on the mass of the people . . . to react in a certain way to certain stimuli. The Russians today are a disciplined, well-trained people; not a happy people, perhaps, but not at all likely to rise up against their rulers."

Eleanor was impressed with the symbol of the dove of peace that appeared everywhere, from the sides of trucks to large posters. But this, she discovered, was only to remind people how hard they must work and sacrifice because their great enemy, the United States, was trying to bring about a war against Russia. The people got only the communist point of view of what was happening in the world, and Eleanor felt "we are going to have to make far greater efforts than in the past if we hope to avoid the war that the Kremlin has told the people over and over and over again that we might start."

Eleanor had to fly to Yalta to see Khrushchev. Mrs. Larova, the interpreter who had also interpreted for the Russians at the Yalta Conference, showed Eleanor the bedroom and study Franklin had occupied. She remembered how much she had wanted to attend that conference and couldn't help wondering if Franklin and Churchill would have conceded so much to Russia if she had been able to influence the decisions. She remembered her victory over Vishinsky at the time of the Declaration of Rights problems.

Khrushchev's villa had a view of the city of Yalta which Eleanor admired. The interview took place on the porch, with Dr. Gurewitsch setting up his tape recorder and Mrs. Larova interpreting the questions and answers. They talked about disarmament, the spread of communism throughout the world, misunderstandings and fear. They talked about the attitude toward the Jews, the problems between Israel and Egypt.

After two and a half hours Khrushchev wanted to tell his papers that they had had a friendly conversation. Eleanor amended, "You can say that we had a friendly conversation but that we differ."

Eleanor reflected afterward that America was involved in much more than a military struggle. She recognized that Russia had made great economic strides in improving the lot of the average Russian, and their progress in material benefits might appeal to underdeveloped countries more than words of democracy. "We have to show by our actions that we can live up to the ideals we profess."

Eleanor felt we should offer needy countries the technical know-how "to help them achieve the freedom to eat, and practical help in developing, step by step, a democratic way of life."

The thing that frightened her in Russia was that her country might be too lazy and comfortable to accept the challenge. "We must regain a vision of ourselves as leaders of the world. We must join in an effort to use all knowledge for the good of all human beings. When we do that, we shall have nothing to fear."

But when Eleanor returned to the United States she learned of the Soviet Sputnik, the first breakthrough in space with an artificial satellite. When she was asked whether she thought the Russians wanted war, she answered that the Russians "have made up their minds they can win what they want without war." They wanted coexistence, but on a competitive basis. The task of the United States, she maintained, was to turn it into "cooperative coexistence."

Eleanor made another trip to Russia in 1958 and even entertained Khrushchev at Hyde Park when he came to the United States in 1960, despite the fact that she thought he had acted "outrageously" by his notorious act of banging his shoe on the table at the U.N. to disparage the United States.

In the pre-election days of 1960 Eleanor did not endorse any candidate until it became obvious to her that there was a strong underground movement to draft Stevenson for a third attempt at the Presidency. But Stevenson hung back, saying publicly he was not a candidate. Yet he also said he would serve his country and his party if called upon.

James, Franklin, and Elliott had all endorsed John Kennedy, but Eleanor felt he had not had enough experience in foreign affairs. She liked vice-presidential running mate Lyndon Johnson's ability to get the civil rights bill to a vote.

But Eleanor finally decided that a Stevenson-Kennedy ticket would win the election and found herself plunged into the middle of the campaign to have Stevenson nominated.

Despite all she could do by speeches, letters, and telegrams to delegates, Kennedy was nominated on the first ballot, and Eleanor left the convention unhappy with the outcome and wondering what might have been done differently. Perhaps Stevenson should have been more decisive.

But when Kennedy asked to see her, Eleanore received him at Hyde Park for lunch and wrote to a friend afterward that the difficulties of the campaign had seemed to mature him and that he truly was interested "in helping the people of his country and mankind in general." She agreed to work in his campaign.

When he was elected after a close contest against Richard M. Nixon, Eleanor wrote in "My Day" that she thought Kennedy had the qualities of confidence and optimism and a mind "flexible enough to be willing to try new approaches." She was sure he would make a fine President.

He asked for her advice and she gave it freely, writing him frequently. She sent him a list of women she considered eligible for high positions; she thought the press conference questions were too sophisticated for the average man to understand and suggested Fireside talks directly to the

American people as Franklin had done; she even suggested he take a few voice lessons to learn how to put more warmth into his television speeches.

Eleanor hoped Kennedy would not abandon hopes of negotiation with the Russians. She was in favor of a demilitarized zone in central Europe. She wrote Jackie Kennedy about the difficulties she would face as First Lady and complimented her on having "a high order of intelligence, self-discipline, and a dedication to the public good."

Eleanor's family warned her she was attempting to do too much at her age. She was still lecturing, writing books, articles, her column for the newspapers and for *McCall's* magazine, traveling, becoming a professor at Brandeis University, entertaining guests at the Val-Kill cottage and for dinner at her New York apartment, and remembering her friends' birthdays and anniversaries.

On her 77th birthday Eleanor said, "I suppose I should slow down, . . . but I could not be content at any age to take my place in a corner by the fireside and look on . . . I feel it's a necessity to be doing something which you feel is helpful in order to grow old gracefully."

But time was running out for the great lady. Her doctor, David Gurewitsch, had diagnosed the various chills, aches and fevers she had tried to ignore as aplastic anemia, a failure of the bone marrow to form blood. But in February of 1962 Eleanor went to Europe to work on a television series, "Prospects of Mankind." She remembered her honeymoon there fifty-seven years ago. She also found time to have lunch with some of her Allenswood classmates she had kept in touch with, and to go sleighing at St. Moritz in the Swiss Alps.

But Eleanor's energy came and went, leaving her weary. She was often in pain which she tried to ignore by sheer will power. In July she entered the hospital for tests and injections, and decided if that was the best life had to offer now, "is it really worth it?"

When she left the hospital she told her housekeeper at Hyde Park there would be no more big parties. But there would be fourteen for breakfast. Against her doctor's protests, she flew to Campobello for the dedication of the FDR Memorial Bridge linking the island with the mainland. She drove back with Joseph Lash's wife Trude, down the Maine coast, stopping to see friends, but sometimes feeling too weak to get out of the car.

Back home again, Eleanore dictated in a whispery voice to her secretary, "This I believe with all my heart. If we want a free and peaceful world, if we want to make the deserts bloom and man grow to greater dignity as a human being, we can do it!"

Where did this conviction come from? From Mlle. Souvestre so many years ago? From her own struggle to cast aside the shackles of self-doubt and emerge as a free and independent woman? From her own need for love and her recognition that it was a universal need that must be met? From what success she had had in promoting the necessity for world understanding? She was optimistic about the future.

Eleanor tried to keep on doing things she had always done. It was painful to get in and out of cars, but she went to the AAUN's reception for the U.S. delegation to the 1962 General Assembly, sitting on the dias for two hours.

At the end of September she had to be hospitalized again and returned home on October 18. Her seventy-eighth birthday on October 11 occurred while she was in the hospital, but she had ordered a birthday party for her grandchildren and the children of friends.

Eleanor grew steadily weaker, however, despite oxygen,

injections, and medications she often refused. Her heart finally stopped on November 7. She accepted death as she had accepted life, doing the best she was able to do. As she had said, "You have to accept whatever comes and the only important thing is that you meet it with courage and with the best that you have to give."

Eleanor had also said, "One must never, for whatever reason, turn his back on life . . . the thing I am most grateful about is for an interesting life, and the opportunities I had to learn along the way."

The funeral was held at St. James' Church, Hyde Park, with burial in the rose garden beside Franklin. A President, two ex-Presidents and the Vice-President and their families attended; 250 people had lunch at Stone Cottage. Memorial services were held also in New York's Cathedral of St. John the Divine and in the Washington Cathedral.

Adlai Stevenson, speaking to more than ten thousand people in New York, said, "She would rather light a candle than curse the darkness."

Ten years later, at the dedication of the new Eleanor Roosevelt wing of the Roosevelt Museum and Library, this statement would be etched in glass on the base of a Steuben crystal flame that enclosed uplifted hands. A tribute to her read:

The glowing radiance of her smile reflected the flame she carried in her heart for the betterment of mankind and the alleviation of human misery.

Her courage led her to new and heroic endeavor in grappling with the pressing problems of hunger, disease and poverty.

The National Conference on Social Welfare is humble and grateful that she has passed among us and shared her ideals with us. We will be ever mindful of the ideals she has set before us.

Her indomitable spirit lives on to inspire those who strive to follow the pathways she has opened.

Eleanor Roosevelt Said:

One of the things I believe life intends us to learn is an adaptability to the new requirements that may come to us at any moment.

Varieties of working experience are good for us all.

My own life has been crowded with activity, and best of all, with people.

I always have a sense that public occasions of any kind are not times during which you live; they are just times which you live through.

Either we are strong enough to live as a free people, or we will become a police state.

You can't talk civil rights to people who are hungry.

Unless time is good for something, it is good for nothing.

A woman's will is the strongest thing in the world.

A man who chooses to hold public office must learn to accept the slander as part of the job and to trust that the majority of the people will judge him by his accomplishments in the public service.

Self knowledge is the ability to look at oneself honestly. Until you can do that, you can't understand or be sympathetic with others.

Nothing we do is ever wasted; if it is good, it will serve some good purpose in the future; if evil it may haunt or handicap our efforts in unimagined ways.

Build a character that can meet new conditions without fear.

No friendship can exist without loyalty.

The final judgment of the worthiness of all human beings is in the hands of God.

About Eleanor Roosevelt:

Her serenity of poise was so great that it gave strength to those about her. Above all, Eleanor Roosevelt was always and essentially womanly, with an understanding of the small and grievous pain of everyday life.

—Dowager Marchioness of Reading

She was a beacon of hope and promise for all those throughout the world who are underprivileged and discriminated against, oppressed and victimized by forces of prejudice and greed.

—Ralph Bunche

Millions of people all over the world think of Mrs. Roosevelt as their friend.

—Dag Hammerskjold

She embodied the vision and the will to achieve a world in which all men can walk in peace and dignity.

—Adlai Stevenson

Eleanor Roosevelt's greatest talent, as the world came more and more to see, was her ability to reduce the quarrels of doctrine and dogma to human differences which could be discussed in human terms.

—Archibald MacLeish

A woman who stood for compassion and hope in every continent of the earth. She was a "great lady," but a warm, completely honest, fearless woman who changed the history of our time.

—Archibald MacLeish

Her life was both ordeal and fulfillment. It combined vulnerability and stoicism, pathos and pride, frustration and accomplishment, sadness and happiness . . . a great and gallant—and above all, a profoundly good—lady.

—Arthur M. Schlesinger, Jr.

She made of herself a measure of what could be accomplished if you abided by your principles and held on to your faith. Idealism as she practiced it had proved its worth in human affairs.

—Elliott Roosevelt

Bibliography

Asbell, Bernard, "Mother and Daughter, the Letters of Eleanor and Daughter," N.Y., Coward, McCann & Geoghegan, 1982.

Asbell, Benard, "The F. D. R. Memoirs," N.Y., Doubleday, 1973.

Beasley, Maurine H., "Eleanor Roosevelt and the Media, A Public quest for Self Fulfillment," Univ. of Ill. Press, 1987.

Berger, Jason, "A New Deal for the World, Eleanor Roosevelt and American Foreign Policy," Brooklyn College, 1981.

Bishop, Jim, "FDR's Last Year," N.Y., William Morrow & Co., 1974.

Cook, Blanche Wiesen, "Eleanor Roosevelt, 1884–1933," N.Y., Viking Penguin, 1992.

David, Kenneth S., "FDR: The New Deal Years," Random House, 1986.

Douglas, Helen Gahagan, "The Eleanor Roosevelt We Remember," N.Y., Hill & Wang, 1963.

Dow, Dorothy, "Eleanor Roosevelt, an Eager Spirit," Norton, 1984, Ruth McClure, Editor.

Eaton, Jeannette, "The Story of Eleanor Roosevelt," N.Y., William Morrow & Co., 1956.

Faber, Doris, "The Life of Lorena Hickok, E. R.'s Friend," N.Y., William Morrow & Co., 1980.

Faber, Doris, "Eleanor Roosevelt," N.Y., Viking Penguin, Inc., 1985.

Farr, Finis, "F.D.R.," New Rochelle, N.Y., Arlington House, 1972.

Freidel, "Franklin D. Roosevelt, The Triumph," Boston, Little Brown, 1956.

Gallagher, Hugh Gregory, "FDR's Splendid Deception," N.Y., Dodd Mead, 1985.

Halacy, D. S. Jr., "Encyclopedia of the World's Great Events 1936," Derby, Conn., Monarch Books, 1963.

Hareven, Tamara, "Eleanor Roosevelt, An American Conscience," Da Capo, 1975.

Harrity, Richard, and Ralph G. Martin, "Eleanor Roosevelt, Her Life in Pictures," N.Y., Duell, Sloan & Pierce, 1958.

Harrity, Richard, "The Human Side of FDR," N.Y., Duell, Sloan & Pierce, 1968.

Hickok, Lorena, A., "The Story of Eleanor Roosevelt," N.Y., Grosset & Dunlap, 1959.

Hickok, Lorena, A., "Eleanor Roosevelt, Reluctant First Lady," N.Y., Dodd, Mead, 1962.

Hoff-Wilson, Joan, and Marjorie Lightman, Eds., "Without Precedent, The Life of Eleanor Roosevelt," Indiana Univ. Press, 1987.

Jacobs, William Jay, "Eleanor Roosevelt, a Life of Happiness and Tears," N.Y., Coward, McCann, 1983.

Johnson, Ann D., "The Value of Caring, the Story of Eleanor Roosevelt," Oak Tree Pub., 1977.

Kearney, James, "Anna Eleanor Roosevelt: The Evolution of a Reformer," Boston, Houghton Mifflin, 1968.

Kleeman, Rita Halle, "Gracious Lady: The Life of Sara Delano Roosevelt," N.Y., Appleton-Century, 1935.

Lash, Joseph P., "Eleanor and Franklin," N.Y., W. W. Norton Co., 1971.

Lash, Joseph P., "Eleanor, The Years Alone," N.Y., W. W. Norton Co., 1972.

Lash, Joseph P., "Love, Eleanor," N.Y. Doubleday & Co., 1982.

Lash, Joseph P., "Life Was Meant To Be Lived," A Centenary Portrait of Eleanor Roosevelt, W. W. Norton Co., 1984.

Lash, Joseph P., "A World of Love," Eleanor Roosevelt and Her Friends, N.Y., Doubleday & Co., 1984.

McAulay, Karen, "Eleanor Roosevelt," New Haven, Philadelphia, Chelsea House Pub., 1987.

MacLeish, "The Eleanor Roosevelt Story," Boston, Houghton, Mifflin, 1965.

Richards, Kenneth, "People of Destiny—Eleanor Roosevelt," Chicago, Children's Press, 1968.

Roosevelt, Eleanor, "Hunting Big Game in the Eighties: The Letters of Elliott Roosevelt, Sportsman, Edited by his Daughter," N.Y., Charles Scribner's Sons, 1933.

Roosevelt, Eleanor, "It's Up to the Women," N.Y., Frederick A. Stokes, 1933.

Roosevelt, Eleanor, "This Is My Story," N.Y., Harper & Bros., 1939.

Roosevelt, Eleanor, "If You Ask Me," N.Y., Harper & Bros., 1946.

Roosevelt, Eleanor, "This I Remember," N.Y., Harper & Bros., 1949.

Roosevelt, Eleanor, "It Seems To Me," N.Y., Harper & Bros., 1954.

Roosevelt, Eleanor, "On My Own," N.Y., Harper & Bros., 1958.

Roosevelt, Eleanor, "You Learn By Living," N.Y., Harper & Bros., 1960.

Roosevelt, Eleanor, "Book of Common Sense Etiquette," N.Y., Macmillan, 1962.

Roosevelt, Eleanor, "Tomorrow Is Now," N.Y., Harper & Row, 1963.

Roosevelt, Eleanor, "My Day," 1936–1945, Rochelle Chadakoff, Ed., N.Y., Pharos Books, 1989.

Roosevelt, Eleanor, "My Day," 1945–1952, David Emblidge, Ed., Pharos Books, 1990.

Roosevelt, Eleanor, "My Day," 1953–1962, David Emblidge, Ed., Pharos Books, 1991.

Roosevelt, Elliott, and James Brough, "A Rendezvous With Destiny, The Roosevelts of the White House," G. P. Putnam's Sons, 1975.

Roosevelt, Elliott, and James Brough, "The Roosevelts of Hyde Park," An Untold Story, N.Y. G. P. Putnam's Sons, 1973.

Roosevelt, Elliott, and James Brough, "Mother R, Eleanor Roosevelt's Untold Story," N.Y., G. P. Putnam's Sons, 1977.

Roosevelt, Elliott, and James Brough, "Eleanor Roosevelt With Love, a Centenary Remembrance," N.Y., Lodestar, 1984.

Roosevelt, James, "My Parents, A Differing View," Playboy Press, 1976.

Roosevelt, James, and Sidney Shalett, "Affectionately, F.D.R.," N.Y., Harcourt, Brace, 1959.

Scharf, Louis, "Eleanor Roosevelt, First Lady of American Liberalism," Boston, Twayne Publishers, 1987.

Sherwood, Robert E., "Roosevelt and Hopkins," N.Y., Harper, 1948.

Steeholm, Clara, and Hardy, "The House At Hyde Park," N.Y., Viking, 1950.

Steinberg, Alfred, "Mrs. R., The Life of Eleanor Roosevelt," N.Y., G. P. Putnam's Sons, 1958.

Watrous, Hilda, "In League With Eleanor," Eleanor Roosevelt and the League of Women Voters, L.V.W., N.Y.S., 1984.

Wayne, Bennett, ed., "Women With a Cause," Gerrand, 1975.

Weil, Ann, "Eleanor Roosevelt, Courageous Girl," N.Y., Bobbs Merrill, 1965.

West, J. B., "Upstairs At the White House," N.Y., Coward McCann, 1973.

Whitney, Sharon, "Eleanor Roosevelt," N.Y., Franklin Watts, 1982.

Youngs, William, "Eleanor Roosevelt, A Personal, Public Life," N.Y., Little, 1985.

Youngs, William, "Eleanor Roosevelt," (Large Print Edition), Thorndike Press, 1985.

Articles By Eleanor Roosevelt

"As a Practical idealist," From series "Why Democrats Favor Smith," in the *North American* Review, Nov., 1927.

"Building Character," *Parents Magazine,* June, 1931.

"Conquer Fear and You Will Enjoy Living," *Look,* May 23, 1939.

"I Remember Hyde Park," *McCall's,* Feb. 1963.

"Ideal Education," *The Woman's Journal,* Oct., 1930.

"Jeffersonian Principles: The Issue in 1928," *Current History,* June, 1928.

"The Seven People Who Shaped My Life," *Look,* June 19, 1951.

"Ten Rules For Success in Marriage," *Pictorial Review,* Dec., 1931.

"What I Want Most Out of Life," *Success Magazine,* May, 1927.

"What Kind of Education Do We Want for Our Girls?" *Woman's Journal,* Oct., 1930.

"Wives of Great Men," *Liberty,* 1932.

"Women Have Come a Long Way," *Harper's Magazine,* Oct., 1950.

"Women Must Learn to Play the Game as Men Do," *Redbook Magazine,* April, 1938.

Pamphlet: "Franklin D. Roosevelt and Hyde Park:

Personal Recollections of Eleanor Roosevelt," Washington, D.C., Government Printing Office, 1949.

Index

About The Author

VIRGINIA VEEDER WESTERVELT juggled three careers for several years. She was a professional writer, a teacher and a homemaker, with a husband and two children. She has written six previous books and over a hundred articles, stories, and poetry in a variety of national publications.

She taught high school English in New York State and then in the English Department of the University of Redlands, California, and in Hong Kong College, Hong Kong. Here she began her biography of Pearl Buck, who grew up in China.

Mrs. Westervelt attended Pomona College in California, graduated from Wellesley College in Massachusetts, and received her M.A. degree from Syracuse University in journalism.

She has retired from teaching, but lectures and says she may never retire from writing nor from her extended family, now scattered from Cape Cod to Colorado but kept close by frequent phone calls and visits.

She is a member of the Society of Children's Book Writers and Illustrators, the National League of American Pen Women (Eleanor Roosevelt was an Honorary member of this group), charter member of the Hong Kong Branch of P.E.N. International, several educational and philanthropic organizations, and a Board member of the Friends of the A. K. Smiley Library in Redlands.

She was born in Schenectady, New York, has traveled widely, and now lives in California with an office room on the patio, "cluttered," she says, "with computer, typewriter, six file cabinets, and seven bookcases."